THE MIDDLE OF NOWHERE

BY DENNIS JERNIGAN

SHEPHERD'S HEART MUSIC, INC.

Published by Dennis Jernigan/Shepherd's Heart Music, Inc.

7804 West Fern Mountain Road

Muskogee, OK 74401

No part of this publication may be reproduced in any form without the prior written permission of the publisher except in the case of brief quotations within critical articles and reviews.

©2020 Dennis Jernigan

Jernigan, Dennis: The Middle of Nowhere

ISBN (paperback): 978-1-948772-15-0

ISBN (epub): 978-1-948772-16-7

ISBN (mobi): 978-1-948772-17-4

Cover Design: Jones House Creative

Edited by: Darren Thornberry

All songs (words and music) written by Dennis Jernigan unless otherwise noted.

INTRODUCTION

Why write a book about being in the middle of nowhere? Why now? The simple answer to those questions is this: We can expect moments in life in which we feel stranded in a desert of the soul, adrift on an endless ocean of despair, or clinging by a thread to a small sliver of hope as we are bombarded by a storm of life. We might feel we have no direction or purpose in life; we might feel different, misunderstood, betrayed or abandoned. Or we could be floundering our way through the messiness life can be at times, feeling we are alone in the battles we must face, hopeless and helpless to gain freedom from a besetting sin or bad habit.

I had to come to grips with this many years ago, but it all came to a head again when I was diagnosed with Parkinson's disease on January 28, 2019. Having just gone through the loss of my father on August 31, 2017, and knee replacement in August of 2018, my soul was reeling and careening downward in a spiral of grief, despair, and physical suffering I could not yet understand. I felt trapped in the middle of nowhere on so many levels.

The good news? God had been trying to show me just how near He was to me during those times of painful loneliness and despair. The even better news? He would meet me in the middle of anywhere I could possibly find myself. He wastes nothing we go through. Nothing surprises God and nothing is too big for Him to deal with. In fact, He uses the things that the enemy means for evil…for our good and for His glory!

And the best news of all? We do not go through or face any trial alone because our God goes with us through the fire, through the ocean of despair, through the storm, through the grief, through the physical suffering, through the middle of nowhere. He meets us and loves us right where we are, but loves us enough not to leave us there.

Life will bring afflictions. Life can be crushing at times. Life can be full of confusion as to which way is up and which is down. Life can feel hopeless and meaningless. Life can knock us down. Life can leave us feeling abandoned and persecuted…like a long line of moments where we go from one middle-of-nowhere moment to the next. So how do we break the cycle of feeling defeated and lonely? How do we find the good in the tedious and hard times of life? The Lord never promised us life would be easy. In fact, He calls us to take up our cross and follow Him, but He did promise us He would never leave us or forsake us and that He would use even the worst moments of our lives for our good and for His glory.

2 Corinthians 4:7-11 says, "But we have this treasure in earthen vessels, so that the surpassing greatness of the power will be of God and not from ourselves; we are afflicted in every way, but not crushed; perplexed, but not despairing; persecuted, but not forsaken; struck down, but not destroyed; always carrying about in the body the dying of Jesus, so that the life of Jesus also may be manifested in our body. For we who live are constantly being delivered over to death for Jesus' sake, so that the life of Jesus also may be manifested in our mortal flesh."

The reason for this book? I am not the only one who has

found himself in the middle of nowhere in life. Due to my story of redemption, I hear from countless people who feel alone in the struggle for freedom or hope or love in their lives, and I see the writing of this book as a way to help them find the Answer they need. That Answer? Jesus…simple intimacy with Jesus. In this book, I will be brutally honest about many of the storms and sufferings I have had to endure as a means of helping you find what I have found in those middle-of-nowhere times.

Dennis Jernigan

The Middle Of Nowhere - a 12-song collection:

The initial inspiration for this book actually came from the title track of a recording project called *The Middle of Nowhere*. The 12 songs inspired the last 12 chapters of this book. They are songs that continue to help me get through the rough days of life… songs that remind me I am never alone and that I am very loved. As you listen to each song, may it inspire you to see beyond what the enemy wants you to see and remind you to look at life and its circumstances from our King's point of view. The entire album, *The Middle of Nowhere*, is available on iTunes or at dennisjernigan.com.

1
HOW DID I GET HERE?

"If you could kick the person in the pants responsible for most of your trouble, you wouldn't sit for a month."

— THEODORE ROOSEVELT

"…Seek first His kingdom of God and His righteousness, and all these things will be added to you. So do not worry about tomorrow; for tomorrow will care for itself. Each day has enough trouble of its own."

— JESUS, MATTHEW 6:33-34

What qualifies me to write a book about feeling utterly alone and living life seemingly in the middle of nowhere? I had a stable family life while growing up. I went to college. I have a successful marriage that produced nine amazing children (and their awesome spouses) and—so far—11 incredible grandchildren. I have had a lifetime of successful ministry and have been blessed with an incredible music career that, to this day, reaches around the world. To top it all off, I live on 90 secluded acres in rural northeastern Oklahoma, 16 miles from where I grew up. Most of my city slicker friends tell me I really do live in the middle of nowhere. What they don't know what I hope to communicate with this book—is that, from my point of view, I live in paradise...that paradise can be found in the middle-of-nowhere times of life regardless of our circumstances.

I have shared what I am about to tell you with very few people. My purpose in writing these untold accounts is to help you understand how I came from feeling utterly alone in my life to knowing I am never alone. I have a feeling you will be able to identify with me on many levels. After all, we are all human... and life is hard. Even Jesus acknowledged this when He said, "Each day has enough trouble of its own." The difference between trouble being a debilitating weight around one's neck or being a lifeline to hope is simple. It all boils down to one's point of view. Sin led us into this troubled life. Jesus came to make sense of it all. Focus on ourselves leads to despair and disorientation. Focus on the Solid Rock of Jesus Christ leads to hope and a true sense of purpose and direction...even when we find ourselves in the middle of nowhere. After you read this chapter, see if you think I qualify to speak on such lofty matters...

My life seems to be a paradox at times. According to all the personality tests I have taken, I am a classic introvert. My deepest sense of self is found in time alone spent creating. As I take an honest look at my life, I must confess I am deeply sensitive...intuitive...able to walk into a room and have a sense of who in that room is hurting or sad or depressed. At times I am able to see the world in black or white, but if I am being totally honest, I tend to see the world in tones of grey. I am convinced the Lord made me this way in order to be able to empathize with others. But the grey areas tend to leave one feeling alone in the middle of nowhere, which is why we need God's Word—a Foundation from which to operate—and why we need relationship with others.

I'm the guy who gets to a party and then looks for the corner to hide in so no one will talk to me, yet I find just as deep a sense of self when singing or ministering to a crowd of people. I have learned to accept my personality and counterbalance its negative traits with the reality that I need relationship with others to truly thrive and to truly live the abundant life God has promised me. Life is not easy; I need a guide through the dark times…through the grey times. If not for God's Word, I would be a tangled mess of a man. After many years of following Jesus, the mess has become less tangled and my point of view has become less self-focused, but I still recognize my need for an anchor for my soul, which comes in very handy when I find myself in the middle of nowhere.

The paradox—an introvert who enjoys being alone but needs relationship with others—is that, even though I thrive on being alone in my creativity, as a human being in need of relationship with other human beings, I experience deep times of loneliness. This seems to have been the case from my earliest memories.

As a small boy with a penchant for artistry and self-expression seasoned with a deeply sensitive soul, I could feel what others were feeling. If you were crying, I was sad with you. If you felt betrayed, I felt betrayed with you. If you felt angry, I felt your anger. This deep sensitivity brought with it much joy in a creative sense, but brought much confusion to my thought-life as I tried to navigate those sensitive waters.

I recall drawing a picture for a first grade class assignment and my teacher being so impressed that she promptly tacked it above the chalkboard and bragged about me in front of the entire class. But I had to run from a boy during the next recess who was intent on causing me as much humiliation and physical hurt as he could because he seemed to be jealous of me for the teacher's response to my drawing. What my teacher bestowed on me was a sense of worth. What this boy's reaction bestowed upon me was a sense of shame for using what I thought was an innate talent or gift...a sense of shame for being "me." This left me with one of my first feelings of being trapped in the middle of nowhere.

The very first time I can recall feeling shame, feeling trapped in the middle of nowhere, was when I was confronted in a sexual manner by an adult male. After this incident, I immediately ran to find my mother to tell her what had just happened, but due to the thoughts bombarding my 5-year-old mind, I stopped short of telling her. I withdrew further into myself. What thoughts caused me to turn inside myself? "Why did that man do what he did? Why did he think I would like it? What's wrong with me?" And, yes, a 5-year-old can think those kinds of thoughts. I can still recall them 56 years later.

Being an ultra sensitive, artful boy who loved to dance and hang out with my girl cousins, yet loved to ride horses and play basketball and baseball with the boys, led to many middle-of-nowhere moments during my junior high and high school years. When my male peers in junior high found out that I played the piano and hung out with girls most of the time, I was called "fag" and "queer" more times than I care to remember. During this period in my life, several boys seemed to make it their life's calling to remind me how much of a "queer" I was. As a result, I endured more than my fair share of beatings and humiliation. Physically a male but told constantly I was something less than a man left me feeling stranded in the middle of nowhere.

Moments like these led me to feel shame on a level I did not have any way of dealing with other than to perform my way through life. One of my earliest conscious decisions concerning my identity as a male sounds ludicrous now that I put it in writing. Since I was not physically a female but, according to the other boys, less than a man, I felt I did not have the right to put my hands in my pockets as boys do when hanging out together. I felt such an act would only draw more attention to me, so I simply never put my hands in my pockets. Shame was all I felt, but at least the other boys didn't tease me for trying to act like a man. That is true middle-of-nowhere thinking.

When I was 10, I was already the pianist for our little Baptist church. One Sunday morning after Sunday school, I was playing on the church steps with my brothers and cousins. Gathered nearby was a group of men I respected greatly because they were my mentors and Sunday school teachers and seemed to know God. Even as I played on those steps, I listened for what these men had to say because I longed to be a man like them some day.

Their conversation was about homosexuals and what they thought of them. I had no idea what a homosexual was until I heard one of the men use the word "queer." Hearing that word, I realized that I was a homosexual…that they were talking about me. My conclusion? They knew God. They loved God. They hated homosexuals. Therefore, God must hate me. This is probably the most middle-of-nowhere moment I have ever experienced.

I determined from that point on that no one would ever discover my secret. My goal was to keep it hidden and to perform my way through life. What I discovered was that when I excelled at sports or scholastics or music, the adults never asked questions. All I ever heard was, "Don't you wish your children were like that Jernigan boy?"

My hidden response to that question was always, "You would be so disappointed if your son or daughter were like me." Middle-of-nowhere thinking.

For all four years of high school, I was the starting point guard and, for a couple of those years, the only white player on the basketball team. Being the only white player on the floor when we played other teams made me a target on the court, but my African American friends would never let anyone hurt me. In fact, they helped me make it through high school without being pummeled and ridiculed on a daily basis. Because most of my friends were black, there was a small racist faction of boys in my high school that hated me. I was often called "N-word Lover." I hated that word but loved my black friends while trying to traverse a white-centered world.

Graduating as valedictorian of my senior class (of 12 students!), I was accepted as a student of Oklahoma Baptist University in the fall of 1977. Feeling like a country bumpkin amidst a sea of students from big cities, I felt lost. Although I could not read music, the school leadership recognized my ear for music and placed me in the top theory class. It was such a classic middle-of-nowhere moment for me because the teacher might as well have been speaking Russian or Chinese. I did not understand a word they were saying! Of course, I sat crouched as low in my desk as I possibly could from the back row in an effort to keep from being called upon!

Since I was majoring in music (and, by the way, the first in my family to ever attend college), one of the requirements of that major was to be a part of a choir each semester. How do you become a part of a choir? You audition. Here's how my audition went:

"Mr. Jernigan, would you please take that choral octavo and go to the third page, second score and fifth measure on that page and sing the alto line in your register?"

Needless to say, I did not pass any audition. But never fear. The school had a remedy for such failures. They had a "special" group called The Shawnee Choral Society. When one of my buddies asked which choir I had made, I mumbled, "The Shawnee Choral Society."

Their response? "Aw. That's alright. You'll do better next time." I felt so humiliated at being placed in this choir that I called it by another name during those days. I called my choir The Island of Misfit Toys. I can laugh at it now, but back then I saw it as yet one more middle-of-nowhere moment in my meaningless life.

It was in the midst of such thoughts that I somehow felt I could write music. In fact, there was something deep inside me drawing me to write music. Feeling confident in this inner calling, I went to the head of the Theory and Composition department and said, "I want to declare my major as a songwriter."

The response? "Mr. Jernigan, we only have a few openings in that department and we reserve those openings for people we see that potential in. And we honestly don't see that potential in you." Middle-of-nowhere moment.

Rather than giving up, and because I felt I had to perform well to prove myself to everyone around me, I worked hard at learning all I could about music. It was during those years at OBU that I was introduced to the music of Christian songwriting trailblazers like Keith Green and Annie Herring and heard their stories of God's redeeming love. Somehow, hearing what God had done for them instilled in me a desire to know God like they knew God…and that maybe, just maybe, I could write music like them someday.

Someday was closer than I thought. Rather than living my life from the middle of nowhere, I would soon find a Solid Foundation from which to live my life. I was about to arrive at my final destination!

2
THE SAGA CONTINUES

"A 'no' uttered from the deepest conviction is better than a 'yes' merely uttered to please, or worse, to avoid trouble."

— MAHATMA GANDHI

"To seek trouble - this is not courage, this is madness. Courage is the willingness of man to sensibly face the troubles he cannot avoid."

— ALIJA IZETBEGOVIC

At this point, I am not going to tell you about how God redeemed me from my past and gave me a brand new identity. You can read all about that in my book, *Sing Over Me*. Suffice it to say that on November 7, 1981, God set me free and gave me a new identity and a brand new point of view from which to live my life. Such joy filled my life at that time that I began to overflow with songs. I could not write them fast enough! It felt like my middle-of-nowhere days were finally behind me. Man, was I wrong!

Between 1981 and 1983, God brought so much healing into my life that I finally felt free enough from my past to be married. Melinda and I were married on August 12, 1983, and life was awesome. We were in love. We were making babies right and left. Music was pouring out of my heart. I felt as if I had finally gotten out of the middle of nowhere...that I had finally arrived. Again, man, was I wrong!

Through a series of events, my music was put into the hands of Jeanne Rogers, worship leader for the very popular James Robison Bible conferences of the '80s and '90s. I had made a recording on cassette of some of my songs. Someone had given a copy to Jeanne. Jeanne called me and asked if she could use some of my music for the Bible conferences. I did not know how big a deal that was since I was so far out of the loop of the Christian music world. Jeanne famously told me, "Dennis, there is an anointing on your music...but the production quality of your tape is horrible! It sounds like you're singing with a bunch of crows!" To this day, Melinda and I lovingly refer to that recording (*See the King*) as Dennis and the Crows.

Needless to say, my music began to be used in churches literally all over the world. I was overjoyed! I suddenly felt as if I belonged somewhere and the feelings of floundering around in the middle of nowhere all came to a resting place on the Solid Rock of who I had become—and was still becoming—in Christ. This place of peace and rest would not last long, though. During the month of July 1988, I found myself in a quandary brought on by one of my favorite passages of Scripture: Psalm 107:1-2.

> Oh give thanks to the Lord, for He is good,
>> For His lovingkindness is everlasting.
>> Let the redeemed of the Lord sayso,
>> Whom He has redeemed from the hand of the adversary

The conviction of the Holy Spirit was brought on by one simple phrase from that passage. "Let the redeemed of the Lord say so." As I pondered what that phrase meant, I knew inside the deepest core of my identity what He meant. It was as if the Holy Spirit was saying, "Son, I want you to tell the world what you were redeemed from."

My response? "I will be rejected. I will lose everything. I will be humiliated. Why would you ever want me to do such a thing?"

His response? "If you who have been redeemed don't say what you are redeemed from, how in the world are those trapped within the same bondage ever going to know there is hope?"

Of course, this conversation between the Holy Spirit and me came to a head when He reminded me of John 8:32, which says, "…and you will know the truth, and the truth will make you free." Meaning? The first step toward freedom is my own honest confession. What this revealed to me was that I was allowing the lies of the enemy to dictate my acceptance and admittance of the truth. It was as if for years the enemy had been whispering in my ear, "If anyone finds out what YOUR past was, you will be rejected. You will be humiliated. You will lose everything."

Once again, I found myself trapped in the middle of God's Word to "say so" and the lies of the enemy to "keep silent."

I was overwrought with fear and knew God was not the cause of that fear, so I confided in several trusted friends as to what I thought the Lord was leading me to do: Share my story of freedom from homosexuality in a public manner. Two friends told me they could have no part of such a thing because it would ruin my life and take away any chance at having my music published while two other friends told me that I must trust God with my story and that His grace would be sufficient for me. Again, middle-of-nowhere feelings kept me bound in indecision.

My wife did not even know about my past because I had received counsel from a trusted believer that this type of thing would not be understood by the church and that God had forgotten about my sin once the blood of Jesus had washed it away…and so should I. When Melinda and I got married, we agreed that we both had sinful pasts and that we did not need to know the extent or nature of those pasts. My point? I needed to tell my wife about my past failures before I ever went public. Her response to my honest confession? "Is that all? Now, can I tell you about mine?"

In that moment of honest confession, the intimacy level in our marriage went into the stratosphere! The opposite of what I thought would happen (the loss of my marriage and family) happened. I found a depth of freedom I never thought possible simply by being honest! If Melinda could handle the truth, it no longer mattered to me what anyone else thought.

God had met me in the middle of that middle-of-nowhere place of my life and allowed me to experience a measure of His presence and grace I had never experienced before that time. On a Wednesday evening in July of 1988, I shared my story with my church body and stood at the altar for the next two hours listening to the confessions and gratitude of those who lined up to tell me their stories! This was one of the most profound moments I had ever experienced in the love of Christ and the affirmation of His body, the church. That middle-of-nowhere mentality was being torn apart by God's loving presence!

This brings me back to the part of my story involving Jeanne Rogers and the use of my music at the James Robison Bible conferences. Since his ministry was massive and worldwide, I thought it best to let him know about my past since they were using so much of my music. I did not want to bring reproach or negative attention or harm of any kind to a work of God so I wrote James a letter telling him of my past and that I recommend he stop using my music so as to not damage his good name.

I got a call from a friend a few days after I had sent the letter to James. The friend was frantically telling me to turn on my TV and tune in to Life Outreach with James and Betty Robison. James was reading my letter on national television and I suddenly had a public ministry whether I wanted one or not! Talk about God meeting me in the middle of nowhere! That was one more affirming kiss from God that He used to remind me that He would meet me even in the middle of nowhere.

3
VICTIM OR VICTOR?

"Naysayers have little power over us—unless we give it to them."

— ARIANNA HUFFINGTON

There came a point in my life when I had to decide whether I was going to live as a victim or as a victor. As an introvert, I tended to see the glass half empty rather than half full, but that is not the mindset of a new creation. I discovered I could change the way I think because I always have a choice. Hear me now. I may not always have a choice as to the things that tempt me or a choice of circumstances, but I ALWAYS have a choice as to how I will respond to any given temptation or circumstance. We simply need to learn how to renew our minds—to think the way our God thinks!

Words have power. Think about the power of the spoken Word of God. He spoke and the entire universe came into existence! People will say things to discourage you from time to time. Sin and the lies of the enemy see to that, but more often than not, the words we speak to ourselves means the difference between life and death; encouragement and discouragement; joy and sadness. We are always being attacked by the lies of the enemy, yet we are often doing most of his work for him without even realizing it. Every feeling we have is attached to a thought we have had. What is self-thought? Words we speak to our own mind whether out loud or in our thought life.

> Death and life are in the power of the tongue,
> And those who love it will eat its fruit.
>
> — PROVERBS 18:21

We have the power to change the way we think about ourselves. When God set me free and I began to share my story publicly, the naysayers came out in droves. "Once gay, always gay"…"He'll be back"…"He's just making up a story in order to sell his music"… "He is doing more damage than good by telling people God changed his identity." I considered such words to be spoken curses over my life and identity and learned very quickly that I must speak truth to myself!

How does one do that? In regard to "Once gay, always gay," I simply reminded myself of the work God did on my heart and mind the moment I realized he loved me so much He would die for me. I could never go back to the gay way of thinking because that is no longer who I am. With regard to, "He's just making up a story in order to sell his music," I told myself that my story is my story and nobody has the right to tell me my story is a lie. Besides, if I were going to make up a story to sell my music, I would have come up with something much more dramatic and universal than "I used to be gay!" Regarding the curse that "He is doing more damage than good by telling people God changed his identity," all I have to do is remind myself of the countless number of people who have told me through the years how God used my story to bring them to the place of freedom in their own lives. I also remind myself that, when I was growing up, I always hoped someone would tell about a way out of where I was…and only one ever did. I decided then and there that as long as I thought there were others in bondage to a false identity, I would tell my story. That's middle-of-nowhere territory these days.

Of course, when God began sending my music around the world and churches began using it in worship, the demand for a recording came about, so I made a simple, poorly produced recording and sold more than 60,000 copies. This caught the attention of three major Christian music labels who all wanted me to sign a deal with them. The pressure to conform began almost immediately as representatives of certain companies wanted to connect me with an image consultant so I would look the look they needed and talk the way they needed in order to sell more records. The pressure was also being put on me to move to Nashville, away from family and friends. I was advised that I needed to be at the center of the Christian music publishing and recording Mecca and that I would need to tour to sell my music.

I chose to not sign with any of them for one simple reason. My first priority was to God. My second was to my wife and children. In fact, it was this pressure to be pulled away from my priorities that helped Melinda and me come up with a simple personal mission statement. "We don't want our children to need a ministry like mine, so I need to be home as much as possible." I only ministered on weekends and always took one or two of my children with me on each ministry trip, each of the nine children on a rotating travel schedule. This meant I would have personal time with each child AND be home during the week.

When I shared this way of thinking with the powers that be in the Christian music publishing business, I was quickly informed that I would not be a viable option for them. One even told me no one would ever sing one of my songs because I needed help with my songwriting...that my songs were too long...that they didn't follow the rules of good songwriting. When I was confronted in this manner, I said, "Our church loves them and many churches in our area use them often in worship."

The response? "Well, that's just your little church. Trust me, that's all the impact your music will have without our help." That's a middle-of-nowhere scenario, but God was right there with me through it all. I walked out of that particular meeting deciding I could not make the concessions they were asking of me.

One good friend in the music business remarked to me one day, "A big part of the issue with you as it regards to the music business is they simply don't know how to market you," meaning not only was my testimony problematic, but the way I held concerts was unconventional. Unconventional? I began almost every worship concert with an admonition to ignore me and focus on the real reason we were gathered. Jesus. Unconventional? At certain points in the "concert," I would ask for people with specific ministry needs to stand, ask people to lay hands on them and pray while I sang a song of deliverance over them—a song from God's point of view. On one occasion, I asked if there were any in the crowd who were contemplating suicide. Over 50 people stood for ministry. Certainly unconventional...in the middle of nowhere!

What happened over the years is quite extraordinary. The Lord seemed to always be there in the middle of my middle-of-nowhere moments, encouraging me to see my life and its circumstances from His point of view. When many were telling me my music would never be useful or marketable, God sent my music around the world anyway. One of my favorite memories of just how uniquely God would work in my life came in the late 1980s. A Word music rep, Rick Carr, was an advocate for me even before I signed a publishing deal with Word Music. Going from

Christian bookstore to Christian bookstore, he would recommend my little simple cassettes along with those he represented on behalf of Word Music! It was Rick who gave my cassette to two men in leadership at Word Music in those days.

Ted Bleymaier, a Word Music executive was one of those men. He tossed the cassette in his briefcase as he walked out the door to catch a flight to Asia on behalf of Word Music. Ted told me he listened to it all the way across the Pacific Ocean and back because there was something special about the focus of the songs. They were songs of intimacy with God. He recognized I had gone through a deeply life-changing encounter with the Lord and told me it came through loudly and clearly in the music in spite of the poor production qualities.

Word Music created a place for me in their publishing and recording market as an independent artist. The reason I signed with Word? Then vice-president (and later, president), Don Cason, was also given a copy of that little cassette and came to the same conclusion Ted had come to. The next thing I knew, both Ted and Don were sitting in one of my monthly nights of praise we used to hold in Oklahoma City on the first Friday of each month (which we did for 15 years) with almost 3,000 in attendance each month. They recognized something I did not even recognize at the time: That God's anointing was what mattered most…that production value was always trumped by intimacy with God. Those three men from Word Music—Rick, Ted, and Don—were used of God greatly in my life. They encouraged me when others discouraged me. They believed in me and the message of my life. In 1993, Don told me to give him the contract points that would make me feel comfortable in signing a publishing deal with Word Music. I did and they agreed! For the next 15 years, Word Music published my music.

In addition to Word Music being my publisher, there were several years in which my recordings were distributed by Here To

Him Music, headed by John Howard. Not only did they distribute my recordings, but their book imprint, Howard Publishing, published two of my devotional books, which sold over 15,000 copies apiece, and published 13 of my songs in the Howard Publishing Hymnal, which is still in use in many Churches of Christ to this day! I will always be grateful for Howard Publishing and Here To Him Music.

In 2008, the music world was changing quickly due to the digital age. That year, I was approached by Debby Berry and Ryan Dahl of PraiseCharts, an online Christian music publishing company. Since Don Cason had recently left Word Music, I felt suddenly alone in the music publishing world and that I was getting left behind in the digital age. Debby and Ryan offered to make my music instantly available to the entire world via the PraiseCharts website. Once my contract with Word had expired, I signed a publishing agreement with PraiseCharts and found a new home. I am honored to be a part of such a world-changing group of people and am very blessed to have them present my music to an entire new generation. Thanks, Charlene Witt, for all you do for the Kingdom and for me!

Through a series of events, I came to serve on the staff at Western Hills Church in Oklahoma City. At first I was janitor for half a day, then secretary for the morning and janitor for the afternoon, and finally worship pastor or lead worshiper, as we liked to say. My job description was simply to sit before the Lord and ask Him if He had any new songs for the body of Christ He would like to create through me. I can't think of a better job! Almost every Monday morning, pastor Jerry Wells and I would meet. He would share what part of God's Word He would be meditating on that week and I would begin meditating on it as well. By the time Sunday morning came, we would often have three or four new songs to teach the body based on those daily meditations.

Following is an excerpt from my book, *Sing Over Me*, detailing how I actually came to be the lead worshiper at Western Hills Church. Melinda and I were introduced to this small inner city body of believers who loved to worship Jesus and fell in love with them. By this time, I had concluded that I would not perform for anyone's acceptance or approval again. Talk about God meeting me in the middle of nowhere!

> Since I was done performing for approval, I felt no need to be a big part of the worship team. For the first year the most I did was an occasional solo. Mostly I was content to play my violin as a simple offering of worship to my God. God was teaching me to find my source of life in Him and not in my performance. Just BEING was truly enough for the first time in my life!
>
> Once Sunday morning, as was our practice as a worship team, we were gathered in a small room next to the sanctuary to pray. The band was there. The praise singers were there. The pastor and the worship leader were there. As we gathered in a circle to begin seeking God together, worship pastor Paul asked to share something. We all respected Paul so much, being such a servant and so loving and encouraging to everyone all the time. But his tone made me think he seemed to be even more solemn and serious than usual.
>
> "God has put it on my heart that I am standing in someone else's place as worship leader. In fact, that person cannot assume their rightful place as long as I am standing in it."
>
> His words felt so heavy to my soul. The entire room felt it at once. The looks on each face said it all. "Paul is resigning and we are about to be devastated."
>
> He went on. "And God has shown me who is to be standing in this place instead of me."
>
> We were all in shock by this point...but my shock turned to disbelief with his next sentence.
>
> "That person is Dennis Jernigan."

Like being slammed with a baseball bat to my head, I was stunned. Before I could even respond, Pastor Jerry chimed in. "God has spoken the same thing to me. And you are to begin today."

Like a deer caught in headlights, I walked zombie-like to the podium, stood, and directed the songs that had already been selected for the service. Though I loved all the songs and felt them wholeheartedly, they did not express what I felt that day. Immediately after the service, I went to pastor Jerry and said, "If this is truly God's will, then I must lead out of my giftings. Let me lead from the piano next week. In that way, I can flow from song to song as the Spirit leads. That was 1986. I have not gotten up from the piano since!

My ministry there actually grew out of our prayer ministry. I began attending these prayer gatherings in 1985, and by 1986 the above scenario had taken place. Monday through Friday each week, from 6:00 to 7:00 each morning, we would meet for corporate prayer. My job was to lead those times from the piano using the Lord's Prayer as the road map to those prayer gatherings. We would begin with worship...Our Father who is in heaven, hallowed be Your name...and then I would encourage the people to pray for God's kingdom to come in their personal lives, their family lives, the local government, the national government, and the world at large. We would worship out of that segment and I would then encourage the people to pray the next portion of the prayer. Worship was the cohesive link between each portion of the Lord's Prayer, and we often did not have time to get all the way through in a single hour. Very often, we would have over 100 people praying in the sanctuary!

In 1993, after much thought and prayer, I stepped down from the position I had held for almost eight years as worship pastor or lead worshiper of Western Hills Church in Oklahoma City. Due to the national exposure of my story via the ministry of James Robison, it was becoming apparent to both Melinda and me that it was time to spread our wings and fly…that it was time to share my story and music wherever God would lead. So I stepped down from my position and moved my family to the farm where I had grown up in Boynton, Oklahoma—a town of less than 500 people. Many would ask why I had chosen to move to the middle of nowhere…

4

BUT WAIT! THERE'S MORE!

"Each of us may think we know exactly what we need to make us happy, what will be good for us, what will ensure we have our happy ending, but life rarely works out in the way we expect, and our happy ending may have all sorts of unexpected twists and turns, be shaped in all sorts of unexpected ways."

— JANE GREEN

"Life is not what you expect: it is made up of the most unexpected twists and turns."

— ILAIYARAAJA

As I look back on my life, it is quite easy to see the very specific plan of God, but it wasn't so easy to see it when going through the steps in that plan as they were taking place. It is those unexpected twists and turns that often leave us feeling used up, broken beyond repair, worn out and weary, and stuck in the middle of nowhere. It is those very same moments, when seen from the

20/20 vision of hindsight, that allow us to see the working out of God's plan…the most profound declaration of truth as expressed in Romans 8:28:

> And we know that God causes all things to work together for good to those who love God, to those who are called according to His purpose.

In 1994, Melinda gave birth to our twin sons, Asa and Ezra. They came nine weeks early. Asa weighed 2 pounds, 7 ounces, while Ezra weighed in at 3 pounds, 10 ounces. The very emotional process of the birth of those boys was made much more bearable by the sheer number of people we had at the hospital, both family and friends, praying for us and caring for us. But the middle-of-nowhere moment came after the boys were sent to the NICU…after everybody had gone home…when the doctor came with the news.

After the birth of our boys, Melinda grew weaker and weaker by the moment. She had no desire to see the boys, which should have been a clue to me that something was very wrong. This was so unlike the woman who had given birth to seven children before the twins were conceived. Her usual reaction after each birth was to reach for that baby and hold him or her as close to herself as she could and not let them out of her sight. After the birth of the twins, she had not been given the opportunity to hold them because of their premature nature, but the room where Melinda was moved after the birth was equipped with closed circuit TV with cameras focused on the babies. Melinda was not interested, and this concerned me.

In addition, her abdomen swelled so much that it looked like she was about to give birth to triplets. Showing grave concern, the doctor ordered an ultrasound be performed. Thinking she would have the nurses wheel her to the ultrasound/radiation room of the hospital, we knew something was not right when the doctor gave the order to perform the procedure in the room as it was too risky to move Melinda. When I asked what was going on, the doctor simply said, "She seems to be bleeding internally. We need to find out what's going on." Within seconds, the team of ultrasound technicians hurriedly rushed into the room with a portable ultrasound unit. While the doctor gently ran the wand over Melinda's distended abdomen, her demeanor grew grave, adding to the tension in the room. She ordered the nursing staff to swaddle Melinda as tightly as possible to constrict her abdomen. Then we were ushered into the middle of nowhere when the doctor turned to us and said, "Melinda, your liver is hemorrhaging and there's nothing we can do. If you're praying people, I suggest you pray right now because she is not going to make it through the night. Mr. Jernigan, I suggest you call her parents." Then she abruptly walked out of the room, leaving us both stunned in disbelief.

It was like watching my wife going over a waterfall. I felt utterly helpless and alone. This all took place in the early morning hours so everyone on our support team had long gone to bed. Melinda closed her eyes and appeared to be slipping away from me. I began to sob uncontrollably, feeling completely emotionally drained, not a mighty warrior of God. As I wept, Melinda came out of her silence and said, "Can you please leave the room? You're annoying me. I need to concentrate and be still. You are not helping..."

Leaving the room, I stopped just outside the door and cried out, "Father, what do I do?" In that very moment, I heard a still, small voice say, "I save your tears when you cry...so cry." My thought at that moment? *What good are my tears when my wife is dying? Why would You save my tears, Lord?* Dragging myself out of my numb stupor, I walked past the nurse's station where two liver specialists were introduced to me, explaining they were poring through medical journals to see if they might be able to find a solution to Melinda's bleeding liver. They offered little hope. Melinda was in the middle of a life-and-death nowhere and I was asking God for the grace to help me call her parents and break the news to them. But then... Walking in the hallway to find a phone, I was suddenly stopped by a nurse who asked me, "Are you Dennis Jernigan?" I told her I was. She went on to say, "I normally do not work this station at the hospital, but when I am called in, as I was tonight, I know God has something special for me to do. He has told me to tell you three things. First, you need to know there are people literally all around the nation lifting your wife and babies up in prayer right now. Second, you need to know your wife is being healed and will be all right. And one more thing—it may not make much sense to you right now—but Father wants me to tell you He saves your tears when you cry."

I lost it all over again, sobbing at the precision and timing of God's Word and presence to our life in just the right moment, in the middle of nowhere. After making the call to Melinda's parents, I quietly crept back into Melinda's room and silently prayed over her. Then I went and found a quiet place and a Bible and began searching for any reference to God saving my tears. Here's what I found:

> You have taken account of my wanderings; Put my tears in Your bottle. Are they not in Your book? Then my enemies will turn back in the day when I call; This I know, that God is for me.
>
> — PSALM 56:8-9

What God showed me as I meditated on those words was this. He wastes nothing. Not even our tears. In fact, He spoke to my heart, telling me that the tears I was shedding were a language of prayer that takes place when one has used all their words. The groaning of my heart became like weapons of warfare issuing out of my heart. God was using my tears to say what my words could not. God was using my tears to turn back the enemy—the liar—and to remind me that He could handle anything I could throw His way, that He was with me and that He was for me.

While God was speaking comfort to my soul, little did I know that He was doing the same for my wife. She told me later what she had experienced during those early morning hours. Melinda had a miraculous encounter with the Holy Spirit. As she felt her life ebbing away, she said to the Lord, "Father, I am ready to be in Your presence." The Lord's response? "No, Melinda. I am coming to be in YOUR presence." She went on to tell me how she sensed the very presence of God holding her and healing her and that she smelled—SMELLED—the beautiful fragrance of God's presence with her. This all took place on Friday night, July 15, and into the wee early morning hours of Saturday, July 16, 1994. By Sunday morning, she began to make a dramatic physical turnaround. We were told she had lost so much blood internally that the pressure of the blood that had built up in her abdomen actually put enough pressure on the liver to stop the bleeding! They gave her two units of blood. Melinda's skin that had paled from all the blood loss suddenly began to grow pink and full of life as those units of blood flowed into and through her veins. She said she could actually feel the life returning to her as the blood entered her body, reminding us that God's Word is true, that there is life in the blood. He wastes nothing and He is with us in the middle of nowhere.

After seven weeks in the NICU, our boys came home. It took several bedridden months at home for Melinda to finally recuperate from the near-death experience and trauma to her body. Once the new year (1995) came around, Melinda was well on her way to complete healing and even felt good enough to take part in our upcoming event in Crested Butte, Colorado, called The

Worship and Ski Retreat. I had learned to ski in college and wanted my children to learn. The family joke became, "If you want Dennis Jernigan to minister in your area, just invite him to a ski area during the ski season." Reality was that skiing was expensive and a large family is expensive but we could accomplish the combining of my three greatest loves in life at that time—family, worship, and skiing—and be able to afford such a trip! The year before, our first worship and ski retreat had been a huge success. The premise of the retreat? Ski all day and enjoy the majesty of God's creation and worship for several hours each night. The second year found us with all nine of our children together in a small hotel on the outskirts of Crested Butte. We booked and filled the entire hotel with people who had a heart for worship. The church that hosted the event and allowed us the use of their facilities was called Oh Be Joyful Baptist Church. Oh Be Joyful was the name of one of the mountains in the area and, thus, a very appropriate name for the church!

The week had gone far above and beyond my expectations. The skiing was great; I believe we had the five older children skiing with us each day while the next two were in ski lessons, leaving the infant twins in the care of a teenaged girl from our church. It seemed the times of worship grew exponentially sweeter and longer with each passing night. I felt as if I were in heaven for the entire week…until that feeling came crashing down quite literally.

It had snowed most of Wednesday night of that week. Thursday was to be our last day of skiing so our family had planned to meet at the top of the chair lift and have our family picture taken. Once at the top, we took an amazing picture that I still treasure to this day and then we had a talk with the children about how to ski in 12 inches of freshly fallen powder. After the safety talk, Melinda headed slowly down the mountain and the children were to follow her in a single line separated from one another by 20 feet or so. My job was to bring up the rear and to help any stragglers along the way. This worked quite well for the first five minutes. As I came over the first gentle rise of the next hill, all I could hear was someone yelling, "Dennis! Get over here! Melinda is hurt!" Speeding down to where my wife lay crumpled in the snow and writhing and screaming in pain, I could see her left leg pinned in an unnatural position beneath her body. It had all happened so quickly. Our five-year-old son had scooted ahead of Melinda, out of control in the thick powder. Melinda had swerved to avoid running him over, only to have the tip of her ski catch in the deep snow and cause her leg to be twisted.

It only took about five minutes for the ski patrol to get to her and assess the situation. From their experience, they felt her leg was shattered and that she would need to be placed in a rescue sled and transported down the mountain to the resort clinic. I had watched my wife deliver nine children and had never seen her or heard her in such pain. Some fellow retreat attenders safely escorted the children back to our hotel while I followed the ski patrol and Melinda directly to the clinic.

True story: the attending physician, a female doctor, was the first to see Melinda in the examination room. By this time, Melinda was screaming and writhing in uncontrollable pain, begging the doctor to give her something to ease the pain. The doctor's response? "Oh, it can't possibly hurt that much! Calm down."

Appalled at the lack of empathy, I addressed the doctor with the first thing I could think of without exploding in anger at her insensitivity. "Ma'am. This woman has given birth to nine children. She knows pain. If she says she's in pain, she's in pain! Do something!" The entire clinic staff, who had come to assist the doctor, heard my response and fell into a reverent hush as they realized the severity of pain from someone who had given birth nine times. The doctor humbly replied, "Get this woman some morphine. Now!"

Melinda responded to the morphine and finally received some comfort. They then took x-rays of her leg. The doctor called me aside to look at them. Her leg, just below her knee, had shattered in a spiral fracture. I told the doctor we were from Oklahoma, that we had all nine children with us and that I would like to arrange for Melinda to be transported to Oklahoma so we could be closer to help from family and friends. She looked at me and said, "Mr. Jernigan, I would recommend you have the surgery she requires right here. Some of the best orthopedic surgeons in the world are in nearby Montrose and they deal with these types of injuries hundreds of times a year."

I still felt it would be in the best interest of our family to have her transported back to Oklahoma. At this point, the doctor referred me back to the x-rays and said, "See these? These are small bone fragments littering her leg. When her bone shattered, it sent shards of small pieces of her bone into the surrounding flesh. What this means is that we risk further damage by moving her such a long distance. My fear is that these small fragments could cause her to hemorrhage. This could mean the difference between life and death for her. My recommendation is that you transfer her by ambulance for immediate emergency surgery in Montrose. I have already made arrangements for her to be moved and for surgery to be performed as soon as possible."

All I heard was the dreaded "h" word spoken only a few months before when her liver had hemorrhaged and all I could see was my wife, once again, near death. And I will never forget the phone call I had to make to Melinda's mother, asking her if she could come to Colorado and help me with Melinda and the grandkids.

My pastor at that time, Chuck Angel, accompanied me for the two-hour drive to Montrose, following the ambulance the entire way. Melinda was immediately prepped for surgery. The procedure lasted almost eight hours and required a six-inch bone graft to be harvested from her hip and grafted onto her shattered bone. In addition, they reinforced the graft with two six-inch-by-one-inch metal plates—one on each side of the break—and 12 screws. After Melinda's mom made it to Montrose, I knew I had to get the kids out of that hotel in Montrose and back to Oklahoma. My amazing mother-in-law, Sheila, assured me she would watch over Melinda while I drove the children home and that she would accompany her daughter back to Oklahoma once she was released from the hospital. Melinda was in the hospital for nine days and the trip home was dreadful. Traveling from a small airport such as the one in Montrose means one boards the plane by stairs from the ground. Melinda had to be carried up the steps in a special chair and then seated awkwardly in a small passenger plane. Flying through the mountains to Denver, she then had to be deplaned by stairs and then wheeled to the flight to Tulsa where she was once again subjected to a painful boarding process. She says it was the most horrendous sequence of flights she has ever endured. We were so grateful for her mother's assistance.

Meanwhile, it just so happened that before our ski trip, Melinda and I had hired a nanny who was to begin work for us once we were home from the worship and ski retreat. She was hired to help Melinda with the little ones while Melinda homeschooled the older children. Once I arrived back home with all nine children, the nanny arrived for work. When she asked me what her duties were, I simply replied, "Just keep 'em alive!"

Over the next few months, Melinda was once again bedridden. It was so difficult to watch her try to be mom to our kids and wife to me from her bed, but she was required to be extra careful due to the type of trauma she had gone through. It did not take long for us to realize she was languishing in emotional stress and feeling absolutely helpless and alone. Absolutely in the middle of nowhere. She had wasted away into a wilderness of despair. Melinda is a natural leader, a git 'er done, life is good, glass is half full kind of woman. To watch her slipping away into this wilderness left me feeling confused, frustrated, helpless and alone. After I came to the end of my wits, I cried out to God for wisdom. What wisdom did He speak to me? "Give Melinda an assignment and tell her you need her to fight to get well." So I did. Since my music was providing the bulk of income for the family and since so many people were using it in worship around the world, God breathed an idea into my mind for my wife. Without giving her fair warning, I walked into our bedroom with a keyboard, blank music manuscript paper, and a packet of mechanical pencils. I asked her to sit up and she did so with a look of utter confusion on her face. All I said was, "I need you to come back to me. Your children need you to come back to them. We need you. The world needs you. And Father God has given me a task for you. While you recuperate, I need you to take your eyes off of yourself and focus on the needs of others." I then plopped the keyboard onto her lap and said, "I want you to take 10 of my most popular songs and write a beginner piano book using them as the basis of the book."

After the shock wore off, it was replaced with what I can only describe as hope and purpose. It was as if she had instantly been transported from abject despair, trapped in the middle of nowhere, to the promised land flowing with milk and honey! She worked on that little book for a few weeks and by the time it was completed, she was back to her old self. When I think back on that time, I cannot help but stand in awe of the power of God to bring someone back from the edge of hopelessness. God's truth? Melinda was needed. Melinda had a purpose. Her husband needed her. Her children needed her. God had met her in the middle of nowhere and in the middle of a lifetime's worth of unforeseen twists and turns. He did not waste one moment of what Melinda and our family went through because He is good that way. And through the years, that little beginner's book for piano sold hundreds of copies and Melinda influenced a whole generation to play the piano in worship to God.

Twists and turns have a way of leading us to the place we need to get to: Seeing life from God's point of view. I believe this is true wisdom, worth the heartache and pain and sorrow and suffering of life to find, because our God wastes nothing.

5
TO STAND ALONE

"To be right with God has often meant to be in trouble with men."

— A.W. TOZER

Blessed are those who have been persecuted for the sake of righteousness, for theirs is the kingdom of heaven. Blessed are you when people insult you and persecute you, and falsely say all kinds of evil against you because of Me. Rejoice and be glad, for your reward in heaven is great; for in the same way they persecuted the prophets who were before you.

— MATTHEW 5:10-12

In case you're wondering, I have experienced more than my fair share of personal persecution because of my faith in Christ. What I am about to share with you are some of the most impactful, memorable and hurtful moments of persecution. From phone calls threatening to kill me to letters telling me they hope my children all turn out to be gay, I share to simply express how, even when left standing alone in the fire of persecution from a human standpoint, I have never truly been left alone for even one second because of the presence of God surrounding me in those middle-of-nowhere moments of persecution.

To me, being persecuted means to be silenced by those who disagree with you. Bing.com defines it as "hostility and ill-treatment, especially because of race or political or religious beliefs." Because of my story of deliverance and freedom from homosexuality, I have often experienced both. When one comes face to face with people who genuinely want to harm them or silence them in a physical way, one understands the reality of persecution often faced by the modern-day body of Christ. Some of my most memorable middle-of-nowhere moments have come during times of literal persecution.

In the early 1990s, I was invited to share my story across the U.S. and around the world. From the first time I publicly shared my story at that little inner city church in Oklahoma City way back in 1988 to the many opportunities I was afforded to share in church settings in those early days, I had been spared of most persecution. Of course, I didn't even call some of what I experienced as persecution in those early days simply because I was so naive and so convinced the world would welcome such good news as I had to deliver. After I told my story in 1988, I began receiving phone calls from friends—now former friends—in the gay community saying things like, "You were never gay" or "Who do you think you're fooling? Everyone knows once gay, always gay" or "Mark my word. You will be back." I brushed those calls off easily enough and thought little of them until the night I received my first death threat. The voice on the other end of that call said, "You're gonna die. Stop telling your story or you're dead." After that particular call, I decided it would be best to have an unlisted number! Again, I thought such non-face-to-face encounters only proved the cowardice on the part of those callers and gave them very little thought until…

In the early 1990s, I was asked to lead a night of worship on the campus of the University of Southern Illinois. My naivety was shattered into reality when I approached the on-campus venue only to be greeted by several dozen gays and lesbians holding signs that declared things like, "Jernigan preaches hate!" and "God loves queers" and "Intolerance will not be tolerated" along with a myriad of other pithy pronouncements. Having never been confronted on such a public and personal level before, I did what I thought Jesus would do. I went to the protestors and asked them to join us for worship and to hear my story. Assuring them that I was hearing what they had to say and that I loved them no matter what, I invited them to come inside, the only caveat being that they not be disruptive. Surprisingly, they agreed to take part. I will never forget them filing inside and taking their seats near the back, still brandishing their signs. After leading in worship, I shared my story and they remained peaceful and respectful the entire time. Of course, such protests were not always so peaceful or respectful.

Again, in the early 1990s, I was invited to lead a worship concert at the University of North Texas in Denton, Texas. More than 10,000 people showed up to worship and most of them had to walk through picket lines of angry gays and lesbians shouting obscenities at them. My heart was so blessed to hear reports of those who had come to worship Jesus reaching out in kindness to those protestors. Again, no disruption took place during the night of praise.

I consider such moments of protest persecution when the end goal of the protestor is to silence me. What I have come to discover is that most protestors invoke their right to free speech but somehow think mine is null and void if my beliefs do not match their own. In such moments, I tend to feel stranded in the middle of nowhere!

In 1992, I was invited to lead worship for and share my story at the Exodus International Conference in Port Loma, California. I recall the leadership of that conference telling us to be aware that protestors could become agitators and potentially violent. This warning was soon made a reality when, during one of the evening sessions (which I had not attended), the stage was stormed by a group of lesbians screaming obscenities and disrupting the meeting. Although I was fortunate enough to have not witnessed what had happened, I did experience a weird kind of persecution from the conference attendees!

During the three days of the conference, I led worship and ministered during all the main sessions. Of course, I used my own music since that is what I had been asked to do. In those days, some believers preferred I use only hymns. In order to minister to them, I included at least one hymn in each session. What I had not expected was the responses I began to receive from people about the use of hymns.

People began taking me aside after each session to offer advice. "You should use only hymns since most of the people here are used to them. You're turning people off." Believe it or not, I also began to hear from people who told me, "You're using too many hymns. We want to sing intimate songs of worship from your heart." It got so bad that I began avoiding people before and after each session, but they were still able to get to me by placing notes expressing their love of or dislike of the hymns in the offering plates as they were passed during each session! Weird and unexpected middle-of-nowhere moment!

Here's what I did. After the first few sessions, I had had

enough from both sides. At the very next session, I began with this statement. "I am hearing from some of you that I do not sing enough hymns...that I should use only hymns. I am also hearing from some of you that I use too many hymns and that some prefer no hymns at all. Brothers and sisters, I am here to obey God rather than men. God has given me songs born out of my own journey out of same-sex attraction. They are part of the weapons of my warfare. I love the hymns, but I also have a new song in my heart. If you don't want me here, I will leave right now. If you want me to use music other than that which God has given me, you are basically asking me to go into battle using someone else's armor. Just as David refused to go to battle in the armor of King Saul, I refuse to go into battle without the armor with which God has equipped me. Should I go or should I stay?"

The place went eerily silent, and after a few moments of what felt like a holy hush, people began to shout out to me, "Obey God!" and "We love your music!" and "We need the intimacy with Jesus your music brings with it!" and "Don't go!" Of course I stayed and not another person approached me with a song suggestion after that moment. I share that only to give another perspective of what it means to stand alone for Christ even in the body of Christ!

One of my most hurtful moments of persecution came during a Bible conference in Canada. I was invited to share my music and to tell my story to several thousand in attendance. Just as I was walking toward the platform during my introduction, a man approached me and began by telling me he had a warning from the Lord for me. His warning? "You are doing more damage than good by telling people they don't have to be gay. You must stop sharing such nonsense." Middle-of-nowhere moment...

I was flabbergasted. Part of my nature in Christ is that I have a merciful heart. I am very empathetic with the pain of others. My first response toward a hurting person is that I tend to feel hurt with them and for them. Because of this part of my character, I immediately began to question myself and whether I should share what I had planned to share. As my name was being announced and I was being welcomed to the stage, I felt dread and turmoil and silently begged God to show me what to do in that moment. Something—Someone—came over me.

I realized that everyone had seen the man take me aside as I was walking to the platform. It was very evident something emotional had transpired in that interchange. I felt humiliated and shamed for a few seconds. Taking my place at the piano, I gathered my wits about me and said, "I am assuming everyone just saw that man (I pointed to him) take me aside. He told me I was doing more damage than good by telling people they don't have to be gay and that I must stop sharing such nonsense." The audience gasped. I continued, "I need to know if that is what you believe. My understanding was that I had been invited here specifically to tell my story. But if I am doing more damage than good, I will step down from this stage right now and go back home. What would you have me do?" Just as had happened in San Diego/Point Loma, people began to shout emphatic words of encouragement toward me and a group of others escorted the man who had confronted me from the building. I shared my story and many, many responded and received freedom in their lives.

In 2001, I was invited to share my story at an outdoor venue on the campus of Oklahoma State University. Having just gone through the physical ordeal of severing my Achilles tendon and having it reattached, I was on crutches and very emotionally vulnerable. It was a cool, crisp fall night and the stars were shining. After leading a few songs of worship, I began to share my story. Near the back of the venue stood a large contingency of the university LGBTQ alliance. Sharing was easy on one hand because I knew I would not have been invited had there not been a need, but it was made difficult at the same time due to the 40 or so protestors mocking and jeering the entire time I was speaking. I recall feeling God was with me in spite of the many attempts to silence me that night. Little did I know how very real His presence was with me.

After my presentation, I stood from the keyboard and took my crutches and made my way down from the platform to greet those who wanted to speak with me. It is my custom to stay until the last person has spoken to me. Even when I am weary and worn out from sharing, the least I can do is acknowledge and value those who need to talk by giving them the freedom to share their own stories or needs with me. As the last person said their goodbye and expressed their gratitude, I was approached by two young men who introduced themselves as those in leadership of the LGBTQ alliance. In no uncertain terms, they began to berate me and mock me for daring to share what I had just shared. The more agitated they became, the closer they came to me. It was obvious they were trying to intimidate me and bully me into silence. I could feel fear rising up within me because I felt alone and threatened the closer they came so I silently cried out to God to rescue me.

In that moment, both young men grew silent and began to back away from me, their faces suddenly having grown ashen as if they were in fear themselves. I heard a voice behind me and directly over my head ask, "Is everything alright, Mr. Jernigan?" Turning awkwardly around on my crutches, I saw the face of one of the star players (whose name I will not mention in order to protect him from public scorn) from the Oklahoma State Cowboys football team. At 6' 5", he was quite the imposing figure who stepped in to rescue me. He firmly told the two young men to back off and stop trying to intimidate me and that I had every right to share my story. In that moment, I didn't feel alone in the middle of nowhere!

Just a few months after that incident, I was invited to New York City for a special event to help launch a ministry to those who struggled with unwanted same-sex attractions, to minister to the families of those who lost loved ones in the 9/11 attacks, and to minister to the police, firefighters and EMS workers. The events of 9/11 had taken place only four months earlier. Before I took the trip, the local newspaper ran a story on my upcoming ministry. The interview was a very positive experience because it made me feel a sense of mission as a representative of our little town to a group of people literally at the front and center of the world's attention.

This was such a special trip for me because I got to take my dad and mom and my daughter, Galen, with me. The effects of 9/11 were still evident everywhere, from the feeling of corporate shock still permeating the city to the still-ongoing efforts to recover the bodies of victims from the twin towers of the World Trade Center. As we visited the site of the tower, there was still much debris and the faint smell of jet fuel. Seeing and experiencing the devastation firsthand made my heart very focused on the needs of the people of the city.

Before I go on, I must tell you one funny story about my mom. This was her first time to fly and my dad's second time. Of course, my daughter had flown dozens of times in her short life due to her many ministry trips with me. Our itinerary was to fly from Tulsa to Dallas and from Dallas to NYC. Boarding a small regional jet from Tulsa to Dallas, we were off. My mom was so excited and full of questions. After a few minutes, Galen got up from her seat and made her way to the lavatory. As she opened the lavatory door, the light emanating from the restroom caught my mom's attention. Concerned with confusion over why Galen had suddenly left her seat, my mom leaned over to me and said in a panic, "Dennis! Galen just went outside!" I could not stop laughing. After a few seconds, I asked my mom, "Mom, think about what you just said. Do you really think Galen could possibly actually go outside of a plane traveling at 400 miles per hour?" I then explained that Galen had simply gone to the bathroom. What an awesome memory from a trip full of awesome memories.

During the several days we were in the city for different ministry opportunities, we toured all over Manhattan. Dad was confined to a wheelchair so I pushed him while Galen and my mom led the way from Central Park to FAO Schwartz; from Rockefeller Center to Grand Central Station; from the Statue of Liberty to Times Square; from the Empire State Building to the Chrysler Building...and many other sites we just wanted to get a glimpse of. It was truly a gift from the Lord to be able to show my parents around that amazing city.

The ministry time actually took place near the edge of Greenwich Village. The place was packed to capacity. We worshipped. I sang over those who had lost loved ones. I sang over the first responders. I shared my story and asked all those who had a desire to walk out of a homosexual identity and into a new identity in Christ to stand. And I sang over them...all 15 of them! It was such a sweet time of ministry and the most amazing part of all? The group that had sponsored the trip used that night to launch their brand new ministry to those who wanted out of the same-sex way of thinking and instantly had 15 people with which to begin! It was an amazing and joyous experience from beginning to end. So, what does such an amazing adventure have to do with feeling trapped in the middle of nowhere?

While on the trip, our local paper's interview with me was published. The very next day, the entire back page of the op-ed section was an article excoriating me and condemning the ministry trip to NYC. Their main point? There was no need to "minister" to people who identified as gay because there is nothing wrong with being gay. In fact, the lead part of the story told how one of the first to die a hero in the attacks on the twin towers was a homosexual priest. The article was meant to humiliate me, to mock me, and to condemn me, but I felt no need to respond.

For the next couple of weeks or so, letters to the editor poured in. Some coming to my defense. Some calling me a fool for believing such drivel. One parent of a homosexual son wrote that she believed homosexuality was normal and that I was doing more damage than good...that I had made up my entire story simply to sell more music! Had I responded, I would have told her that if I were going to make up a story to sell music, I would have chosen a better story than mine! In fact, the Christian music business told me they would have a difficult time selling my music because of my story, often encouraging me to "lose" my story. Talk about feeling trapped in the middle of nowhere?!

In the fall of 2004, I was invited to Washington D.C. to lead worship and share my story at an event called Mayday For Marriage. I led worship and shared with the 50,000+ in attendance. After that experience, I felt so validated and so loved and so relevant! To be a part of such a huge gathering made me feel invincible and a part of the army of God. I could not wait to watch the national news that evening. I should have waited. The coverage that evening consisted of a very liberal explanation of the event, using the words "hateful" and "bigoted" to describe what they assessed to be a less-than-stellar number of people, while focusing almost entirely on the fewer than 50 LGBT protestors huddled somewhere at the side of the huge throng of believers. Middle-of-nowhere moment...

The enemy uses lies to cause us to fear in order to silence us. He uses lies to stir up hatred toward followers of Jesus Christ who dare speak of the possibility of man or woman to change their sexual identity. In July of 2009, I was invited to lead worship and share briefly at the annual Exodus International conference being held that year at Wheaton University in Wheaton, Illinois. After so many years of ministering at conferences and concerts in which it was necessary to be accompanied by armed guards, I admit I sometimes felt anxious about appearing in public, especially in more liberal areas of the nation. That evening, all the doors to the chapel had been locked and were manned by security personnel as I began to share. After only a few minutes, a large crowd gathered in protest outside the main entrance. People began shouting. Horns began blaring. And then the doors were stormed and sounded as if they would cave in from the intense pounding and banging. A moment of dread and panic swept over me but was quickly dispelled when I focused my attention on Jesus and on leading the conference attendees in worship. A very frightening middle-of-nowhere moment.

You might be getting weary of my litany of moments of experiencing persecution. I honestly have tons more I could share, but I want you to know that even when we feel attacked and alone, we are not forgotten or forsaken or short on God's grace. It is in the midst of the fire that Shadrach, Meshach, and Abednego were joined by the Lord Himself. We serve the same God. Bear with me for two more stories…two of my favorite stories…because of the way God showed Himself strong in the midst of the fire.

Sometime around 2008 at a church in North Carolina, I shared my testimony and felt very warmly received and appreciated by the congregation as a whole. As is my custom, I stepped down from the stage to greet people when the service ended. After several minutes, the last person—a very large and imposing giant of a man—stepped up to "greet" me (it's always the ones who wait around the longest who seem to respond with the most vitriol). He began to tear into me with a barrage of derogatory comments ending with the all-too-common "Your ignorance and intolerance are doing more damage than good!" Upon hearing the commotion, the leadership of the church stepped in between us and quickly ushered me out of the building and to a local restaurant for lunch.

After I had calmed down from this unexpected encounter, one of the church leaders came to check on me and asked how I was doing. I explained that I would be fine and that, sadly, I had become accustomed to such encounters. It was no big deal.

She countered my comment with, "Well, it was a big deal to God!" I asked what she meant by that. She went on to tell me that after the man had confronted me and the church leadership had ushered me to safety, something miraculous had taken place. She said that after I had left the auditorium, the man suddenly felt faint and had to be helped to a seat, that he had been unable to recall even having spoken with me, and that he had been unable to drive himself home. As if rendered speechless by the power of the Holy Spirit (Her words, not mine!)! That's New Testament, road to Damascus, middle of nowhere stuff right there!

My favorite memory of persecution (if one can have a favorite painful memory, LOL!) came in December of 2007. I had been invited to perform my Christmas Musical *Hallelujah! Christ Jesus Is Born!* with a church choir and orchestra. At this time, my twin sons were 12 and it was their turn to accompany me for a ministry trip. During the course of the musical presentation, I shared briefly between each song as I felt led. One statement I made with regard to the birth of Jesus, one of the main reasons I love celebrating the advent of Christ, was because of the gift of a new identity He had given me when I was born again, how my mind had been transformed from that of homosexual to that of a heterosexual and how grateful I was to God for the amazing gift of Jesus Christ accompanied by His redeeming, transforming, powerful love. I had taken all of 30 seconds to make that brief statement.

The entire evening was amazing. The choir was full of joy, the orchestra played with zest and power and I felt completely ener-

TO STAND ALONE | 45

gized by the time we were done. The entire congregation stood to its feet in a resounding standing ovation to Jesus! At least, most of them stood.

Once again, I stood at the front of the auditorium, took my place at the foot of the steps and greeted people one by one. The line was quite long that night and the kind words from person after person greatly encouraged my heart. I happened to notice one man who kept giving his place in line to those behind him. I recall thinking to myself, "This man must have quite a story of grace to tell for him to be willing to wait so long."

When the second-to-last person had turned to leave the auditorium, the man who had waited so patiently quickly stepped in front of me and took me very firmly by the hand and squeezed it like a vise. Again, naivety winning the day, I thought to myself, "This man is so grateful and full of emotion. He must have something amazing to share."

Breathing heavily and seething, the man pulled me directly in front of his face, stared me right in the eye and said in the most angry, bitter voice, "You have set the gay community and agenda back thirty years! How dare you tell people they can change… that they need to change!" In that moment, I did the only thing I knew to do. Feeling my life being threatened, I pushed him away from me and shouted, "Get behind me, Satan" and then began yelling at the top of my lungs, "Jesus, help me! Somebody help me!" The stunned church leadership stood by and watched in bewildered confusion. Everything felt as if it were in slow motion. The only ones to move to my defense were my 12-year-old sons. Asa and Ezra came running to me and asked, "What's wrong, dad? What do we need to do?!"

The sound engineer raced from the sound booth and tackled me with a bear hug, almost causing us to fall to the floor. I was appalled and flabbergasted! "I'm not the problem! He is!" I yelled as I motioned my head toward the man who had just confronted me. Needless to say, my sons and I were quite shaken up by this ordeal. Finally, church leadership came between my confronter and me and quickly escorted me to the green room so I could change out of my tux and into my traveling clothes.

Then I asked someone why the church leadership had been so hesitant to come to my assistance. I was quietly told that the man who had confronted me was an important church figure who gave generously to the ministry of this particular church and that they had wanted to avoid any further offenses toward him! Feeling shocked and dismayed, I stepped out of the green room and right into the path of another angry person.

Waiting for me in the church hallway was a very disgruntled woman who flew into me with nothing less than pure rage. She yelled, "I'll have you know I am pastor so-and-so of such-and-such church and I am the sister of the man you just called Satan!" I put my hand up and stopped her before she could go on. All I said was, "Ma'am, I did not call your brother Satan. I was speaking to the spirit of Satan who was deceiving him. I did nothing wrong." With her still berating me, I took my sons and left the premises, wondering to myself why I should ever share my story again. The drive home was anything but peaceful for me. All I could think of was what if that man had done something to injure me in front of my sons or had injured one of my sons? Even though, by faith, I knew I was not alone, I felt alone in yet one more big fat middle-of-nowhere moment.

Peace did come, though. Before we even got home late that night, the Lord reminded me of why I needed to share my story… that if the redeemed of the Lord did not share what they were redeemed from, how in the world would others trapped in the same bondage ever know there was a way out called Jesus? Such truth from the Word of God did much to give me grace to endure so many middle-of-nowhere moments and still does to this day.

Oh give thanks to the Lord, for He is good,
> For His lovingkindness is everlasting.
> Let the redeemed of the Lord say so,
> Whom He has redeemed from the hand of the adversary…

— PSALM 107:1-2

6

THE JAMAICAN AFFAIR

"When Christ calls a man, he bids him come and die."

— DEITRICH BONHOEFFER, THE COST OF DISCIPLESHIP

Many people through the years have expressed their concern for me sharing my story with a world that is violently hostile towards such stories. I have had people ask me why I would even continue to bother with sharing to a world that refuses to listen. All I know is that something deep within me compels me to do so. I have a very good suspicion that it comes from my own past. It is quite easy to recall sitting in church service after church service as a boy and as a teenager, knowing my struggle was a taboo subject to deal with in the church. My greatest desire in those days was for someone to tell me freedom was possible, but no one ever did. I just want to tell those who are out there struggling with unwanted same-sex attraction that freedom IS possible by placing our faith in the Redeemer, Jesus Christ, and by walking intimately with Him, allowing Him to renew our minds. I would rather have not gone through all I have experienced with regard to same-sex attraction…but I have. The writings of Paul to the church in Corinth have helped me understand more of God's perspective on the matter through the years, so much so that I am now honestly able to thank Him for allowing this to transpire in my life.

Because of the surpassing greatness of the revelations, for this reason, to keep me from exalting myself, there was given me a thorn in the flesh, a messenger of Satan to torment me—to keep me from exalting myself! Concerning this I implored the Lord three times that it might leave me. And He has said to me, "My grace is sufficient for you, for power is perfected in weakness." Most gladly, therefore, I will rather boast about my weaknesses, so that the power of Christ may dwell in me (2 Corinthians 12:7-9).

Past failures do not define me. Present temptations do not define me. Circumstances do not define me. Feelings do not define me. Reality is this: God is able to take what the enemy intended for evil in my life and use it for my good and for His glory. I continue to boast about my weaknesses so that the power of Christ may dwell in me so that others in need of hope might receive hope…so that I might not boast in myself. So I had to deal with same-sex attraction. Why not me? So I am having to endure the suffering that goes with Parkinson's. Why not me? So I have had to suffer through and endure the raging vitriol of those who hate me and all I stand for. Why not me? That I might know Him.

The apostle Paul detailed many instances of personal persecution in his letters to the body of Christ. Why would He do so? I believe one of his main objectives in sharing the moments of being beaten, of being imprisoned, and of being publicly mocked and scorned was to encourage the church to be receivers of God's grace and to not be ruled by fear. Here is what he wrote to the Philippian believers:

> But whatever things were gain to me, those things I have counted as loss for the sake of Christ. More than that, I count all things to be loss in view of the surpassing value of knowing Christ Jesus my Lord, for whom I have suffered the loss of all things, and count them but rubbish so that I may gain Christ, and may be found in Him, not having a righteousness of my own derived from the Law, but that which is through faith in Christ, the righteousness which comes from God on the basis of faith, that I may know Him and the power of His resurrection and the fellowship of His sufferings, being conformed to His death; in order that I may attain to the resurrection from the dead.
>
> — PHILIPPIANS 3:7-11

We love the statements about the sufficiency of God's amazing grace, but we balk at phrases that call us into "the fellowship of His sufferings." Who wants to suffer? I don't! I was physically assaulted in high school while being called faggot and queer. I have been publicly ridiculed for daring to say I am now free from homosexuality. I am walking through the valley of the shadow of death in a sense with Parkinson's…yet God has not wasted one single moment of any of those experiences. If anything, God is proving Himself to be present with me in each and every middle-of-nowhere moment of life. As long as we are alive, we will all have to go through middle-of-nowhere moments. May I suggest we do something very simple in preparation? Let us take our eyes off ourselves and fix them on Jesus Christ and on the needs of others, and be prepared to do spiritual battle with the enemy whose only true power is that of deception.

THE JAMAICAN AFFAIR | 51

Be of sober spirit, be on the alert. Your adversary, the devil, prowls around like a roaring lion, seeking someone to devour.

— 1 PETER 5:8

While I believe the enemy prowls around seeking someone to devour, I do not believe he has any teeth! He is a weak adversary when compared to the power of the resurrected King, yet his lies can take us into moments of despair and wound us in ways that may take years to overcome. One such moment in my life occurred in May of 2012. In many ways, I am still reaping the consequences of his lies in spite of my adherence to the truth. I can only be responsible for my own choices and my own responses to those wounds, but I cannot keep others from inflicting them.

In 2008, I was asked to serve on the board of directors for (at that time) the world's largest ministry to those who struggle with unwanted same-sex attraction—Exodus International. It was in those board meetings that I met and rubbed shoulders with some of my personal heroes in the faith. For four years, I was greatly encouraged to feel a part of a worldwide ministry that literally touched and affected millions of lives. It was in the middle of year three of my service that I began to have second thoughts about being a part and prepared to resign my position. Before I could take that step, two other board members tendered their resignations so I felt I needed to stay the course until the board could find replacements for these board members. Little did I know that God had it all worked out. Little did I know of the pain and sorrow and suffering I was about to face.

As the fourth year of my board membership developed, the ministry leadership began making overtures to pro-gay ministries and pro-gay organizations. It was explained that we needed to bridge the gap between Exodus and these groups in order to make inroads toward them with the love of Christ. This began to frighten me a bit but I reasoned expressing the love of Christ to those with opposing views was a good thing. My fright turned to despair when the board president went around to each board member (to those who had come out of the gay lifestyle) and asked them this question. "Do you still feel tempted at times by same-sex attraction?" To a person (myself included), we answered, "Yes, we still have moments where we feel that temptation." His response? "Then nothing has changed. You are still gay."

At that moment I felt absolutely defeated and embarrassed. I believed so resolutely in the ability of the power and love of Christ to transform and change a person's identity only to be told that (my interpretation) change was not possible. I could not stop weeping. I am sure the board thought I was losing my mind, but I suddenly felt utterly alone in the middle of nowhere. In that very moment, I decided two things. I would resign as soon as I could and that I would write my life story (*Sing Over Me*) as a declaration of the truth of my life. Not only was change possible, but I had undergone a complete transformation. I still understood the power of same-sex attraction, but I had changed. One does not forget their past temptations, and one is not able to guard against the constant onslaught of gay propaganda put forth in practically every form of media and entertainment. Yes, I still understand the draw of temptation, but that in no way defines me! I only wish I had spoken up when the question had been posed, but I was in shock and caught off guard in the moment in that meeting. The truth: I was once homosexual, but now I was heterosexual, in spite of my past temptations and in spite of what the board leadership thought.

After I got home from that trip, I told Melinda I needed to resign as a board member but that I needed to give the board time to replace the two members who had just resigned. At that time, we made the decision to wait to resign until after my upcoming shoulder surgery and our ministry trip to Jamaica. The shoulder surgery (right shoulder rotator cuff repair) took place the second week of May. Literally a week later, my right arm in a brace and sling, Melinda and I were in Jamaica…and the ministry was extraordinary on so many levels.

Though in pain and encumbered with a brace, I was able to play the piano and share my story with almost the entire population of Jamaica—two million people! In a four-day period, I publicly shared my entire story 11 times. We went from church to church and from gathering to gathering sharing the changing power of God's redeeming love to thousands and thousands. After each opportunity, I gave an invitation for those who desired freedom to stand while I sang a song of deliverance over them. Hundreds stood.

Melinda and I were so encouraged even though the trip was overwhelmingly exhausting for us due to the surgery and the need for Melinda to do all the heavy lifting of both baggage and my emotional needs. One invitation to share was extended by a nationally-aired talk show known for its liberal bias. I was warned to not accept this invitation because the host was notorious for doing all the talking as well as for catching his guests with "gotcha" questions. I felt I was to accept the opportunity.

No sooner had I been introduced than the host asked me this question. "You say you were once homosexual but are no longer so. How is that possible?" For the next 55 minutes, I shared my story of redemption and transformation on Jamaican national television. My recollection was that the host seemed so taken aback by my boldness and clarity in explanation that he had not been able to cut me off! My perception was that he was genuinely interested in my point of view. Afterwards, our Jamaican ministry host told us he had never seen this particular talk show host rendered utterly speechless. Needless to say,

Melinda and I were beyond encouraged. But that was not to last.

In Jamaica, there are two major national newspapers. On May 21, we were invited to be interviewed by the Jamaica Observer. I was asked to share my story and was received quite well, but then the reporters began to pepper me with questions concerning the laws against homosexuality in Jamaica and what I thought about them. They also asked me what I thought about certain groups who were opposed to pro-gay theology in Jamaica. My response was that I did not feel adequate to speak to their laws, but that I was grateful there were people in the land who were willing to stand alone for the sake of righteousness. Those statements would come back to haunt me soon enough.

The stuff hit the fan when I was asked about then President Obama's public stance concerning his support of gay rights and the push for the legalization of same-sex marriage in the U.S. My response? "I love my president and I pray for my president, but he is deceived when it comes to same-sex marriage." When asked to explain, I simply said, "The family unit—the traditional family unit of one man and one woman—was part of the foundation of our society and that when one messes with or destroys the foundation, the entire structure crumbles and falls apart. President Obama is endangering the foundation of our nation." The front-page headline the next day read something like "Ex-Gay American Says Obama Deceived On Same-sex Marriage." Even though the paper printed my entire story, the headline garnered the most persecution.

I will never forget the phone call I received from the president of Exodus International. I was just coming out of my follow-up appointment with my orthopedic surgeon when the phone rang. The entire conversation took place while sitting in my vehicle in the parking garage of the medical building. The president began, "We need to talk about your recent trip to Jamaica." I was still so pumped at the success of the trip that I totally misread what he was getting at. He went on to say, "You should not have taken that trip without consulting me and the board." I asked him what he meant by that.

"Your public comments and statements have brought too much negative attention to Exodus. This is really bad for us…but it's going to be worse for you. Your reputation is ruined, but we can still repair some of the damage you've done to Exodus. You need to fix this."

In that moment, I felt like lashing out in anger. Since when had I ever had to ask permission to share the Good News of the Gospel of Jesus Christ? Since when had he or the board of directors ever even asked about how my ministry was going? It suddenly felt like I had been used to gain positive public support for Exodus due to the use of my music in churches around the world. I bit my tongue and simply asked, "So you are telling me you want me to resign?"

He answered tersely, "Yes, that would help. Don't make any more public statements. We will handle this on our end. I already have our public relations team drafting your resignation announcement." It went out nationally that afternoon as follows:

In a statement released by Exodus International, the group's president Alan Chambers said:

"Dennis shared his belief that President Obama is deceived about homosexual behavior and the biblical morality of it. Dennis assured me he is not for the criminalization of homosexuality, and he will release his own statement on this matter. However, Jernigan offered this immediate response:"

"I believe my heart and intent were misconstrued and, therefore, may have harmed Exodus' mission of ministering to those struggling with same-sex attraction (SSA). To that end, as of this moment, I step down as Vice Chairman of Exodus."

This was to prove to be one of the biggest and most severe middle-of-nowhere moments of my life. I suddenly went from respected and revered worship leader/song receiver to persona non grata. I felt humiliated and unsupported. I felt betrayed. I felt I had been thrown under the bus. And to top it all off, the next board meeting was only a few weeks later. I, of course, did not attend, but the board called me on a conference call to convey their goodbyes. I cried through the conversation.

After that conversation, the president asked me if I would still consider coming to the national conference in July and leading worship in the morning devotion times. My immediate response was, "I will need the weekend to think and pray about whether or not I can do that." After that call, I simply asked the Lord to give me a sign or some sort of confirmation as to whether I should take part in the conference. The fleece I laid before the Lord was simple. "Lord, if you want me to take part in the conference, have just one board member contact me either by phone or e-mail to check on me over the weekend."

No one contacted me.

I remember feeling numb, confused and wounded, like I was floundering in the middle of nowhere. My wife put it all in exquisitely simple perspective: "At least you don't have to wonder about the right time to resign anymore!"

Sadly, a year later, in June of 2013, Exodus leadership issued a statement of apology to the gay community for having operated out of ignorance for so long and simultaneously closed its doors. Several people asked how I could have been a part of bringing Exodus down. Such assumptions caused me much pain and many sleepless nights. It became easier to distance myself from people than to face such questions. I refused all media requests for interviews and decided to fly under the radar for a while. Yet Father was faithful to me in this very traumatic middle-of-nowhere moment in my life.

On June 26, 2015, the U.S. Supreme Court struck down all state bans on same-sex marriage, legalized it in all 50 states, and required states to honor out-of-state same-sex marriage licenses, in the case Obergefell v. Hodges. As a result of the federal law, churches and para-church organizations stopped inviting me to share my story. One of the largest, most influential churches in the nation had invited me to share my story in one of their healing conferences only to un-invite me a couple of weeks before the event, telling me they needed time to rethink and reevaluate their public stance on same-sex attraction, same-sex marriage, and all gender identity issues. This literally took the wind out of my sails and left me devastated…for a few moments.

Thankfully, a representative of this church sought me out a few months later and asked me to forgive them for the way they had treated me and for silencing my testimony. Subsequently, I was invited back, but honestly, I felt defeated on so many levels even as I shared my story. This was one of the few times in my life and ministry I honestly considered giving up. Naively, I believed nothing worse could ever happen to me. Man, was I wrong.

Let me end this chapter by saying I sincerely and deeply love the people of Jamaica and absolutely felt loved, cherished, and honored to have been in their presence. And while I am at it, I love all people…regardless of how they identify, regardless of their sexuality. Just because I believe God can change any human heart does not mean I am a hater. God loved me right where I was and loved me enough to not leave me there. I can do the same for anyone…even if they disagree with me…even if they hate me…even if they try to silence me…even if they do not see or feel the need to change in any way, shape, or form. I cannot change anyone. Never claimed I could…but with God, I believe all things are possible.

7
TWISTS AND TURNS

"They say that abandonment is a wound that never heals. I say only that an abandoned child never forgets."

— MARIO BALOTELLI

Everyone's life is full of twists and turns. That is just part of life. Change is one thing we can always count on to be consistent in our lives. Change means growth. Growth means maturity. Maturity means we need to give up the hope of ever changing our past because it simply cannot be done, which is wonderful news since we serve the God who never changes. The God who wastes nothing we go through in this life…even times of being misunderstood or persecuted. As I began to write this book, it became abundantly clear that the middle-of-nowhere moments I have experienced have come from a myriad of circumstances and sources, mostly unexpected.

In 1995, God led me to two brothers in Christ who had a vision for starting a new church in our community. During that year, we established several small home groups that met on Wednesday evenings with larger corporate gatherings taking place on Sundays…anywhere we could find to meet. We met in a car wash. We met in a pipe fitters union hall. We met in the YMCA. We met in the civic center. And after only a few years, we built a building. During this time, I was co-worship leader with another friend and Melinda and I led a small group in our home each week. I honestly expected to live out the rest of my days as a part of this body of believers, but that was not to be.

In July of 2000, Vermont became the first state in the union to put forth measures to legalize same-sex civil unions. Since my story was "out there" in the Christian community, a state legislator from Vermont, who happened to be a believer, asked if I would consider coming to Vermont to speak to the state legislature. I agreed to come as long as they allowed me to bring along another brother for support. I assumed it would be easy to find another man from my church to go with me as part of my support team.

Going from man to man, I was consistently met with resounding no after no after no. Each man had an excuse as to why he could not be a part of my mission. To be fair, since they are not able to respond to this personally, as I look back, I can see the reasoning behind all the negative responses and completely understand. But at the time, I felt embarrassed and utterly alone and confused. Embarrassed that I had told my contact in Vermont that it would be easy to find a man to stand with me on the trip and utterly alone in the face of what would prove to be a very difficult trip. Confused at why my awesome brothers seemed to be afraid to stand with me. Did they not think my "cause" was worth fighting for? Unexpected middle-of-nowhere moment…

But there was one who stepped up to the plate for me. After hearing me complaining to Melinda about the lack of support from our church body, my son Israel (who was 15 years old at the time) came to me and said, "Dad, I will go with you." So we went. It just so happened that as soon as we stepped off the plane, we found out the legislature had just passed the bill legalizing same-sex civil unions. As my contact led me into the capitol building, she wanted me to meet the man who had spearheaded the bill. I introduced myself by saying, "Hello, sir. My name is Dennis Jernigan…and I used to be gay. This is my son, Israel. We came to try and persuade you to reconsider the enactment of this bill since it will have a profound impact on the foundation of our society."

As I shook his hand, he became flustered at my words and began to tremble, fumbling for words, and walked hurriedly away. I was immediately ushered into a news conference in which I was peppered with questions regarding my thoughts on what had just taken place in Vermont. I recall feeling so embarrassed at the lack of support and lack of tolerance and lack of compassion, but unashamedly proud to have my son sitting there in front of me in that news conference. Middle-of-nowhere moment but grace upon grace at the presence of my son being with me. I am sad to say that in 2009, same-sex marriage became legal in the state of Vermont. That would prove to be a major middle-of-nowhere moment when I questioned myself and whether I was wasting my breath by telling my story.

My desire is not to paint a picture of poor little persecuted Dennis Jernigan. I share only to express how God's grace is quite available and quite sufficient in and through even the most fiery of trials. Some of my most painful trials have come not as a result of persecution but as a result of conflict with other believers, and I take full responsibility for my moments of walking in something less than love.

As I stated previously in this chapter, in 1995, Melinda and I helped launch a new church body in our community. It was absolutely one of the most joyful 10-year periods of my life. I was co-worship leader with one of my best friends. He would lead when I wasn't in town and I worked as a missionary sent out by the body of Christ. Each week, I made videos for presentation during the announcement portion of our weekly services that would encourage the people to pray for me as a means of helping them be a part of all God was doing through my worship concerts and the sharing of my testimony. My public ministry called me away for two, sometimes three, weekends per month, so these videos helped me stay—feel—connected.

Since the mid 1980s in Oklahoma City, Melinda and I had envisioned our home as a hospital for Jesus, holding weekly small groups and ministering to many people in very personal and unique ways. One-on-one ministry became the bedrock point of view from which we operated as a home and family. Home was ground zero for ministry. The corporate church gatherings were for worship and being equipped to go out into the fields and do the work of ministry. This was such a heavenly time in our lives. My honest thought was that we could live and minister with this body from the time of its inception until the day we died. But that was not to be.

In 2005, our founding pastor felt called away to begin a new work in another city in another state. Since I was on the elder board, I felt a serious gravity to seek God for the next pastor for our body. After many months of searching and seeking, we found our new pastor. I felt that we had found the perfect man who shared the same vision and goals for the church. I wrongly thought that there would not be any major changes.

During the first 10 years of our existence, I was given as much time as I felt led to lead worship during our corporate gatherings. It was not uncommon to worship for 45 minutes to an hour and sometimes longer if we felt the Holy Spirit was moving. I assumed that I would have that same freedom. I was wrong.

After a couple of weeks of me leading worship, the new pastor came to me and asked me to pare the worship down to 15 or 20 minutes at the most. I said I would try, but I failed pretty miserably. My main mistake? Disregarding the pastor's suggestions and leading until I felt the Holy Spirit was done. That sounds incredibly prideful on my part. I should have been more sensitive to what the pastor was trying to accomplish.

It did not take long for conflict to develop. One day, the pastor asked if he could talk with me over coffee. Of course, I agreed. He explained to me that he felt the vision of our church had changed. I asked him to explain what he meant. In a nutshell, he explained that his vision was that our church become a seeker-sensitive church. Since we were going to be sensitive to those seekers, we needed to understand that people needed to feel comfortable and taken care of, and that people could not possibly be expected to stand for more than 20 minutes of worship at a time because it would turn off those seekers who were unaccustomed to long worship sessions.

My response was simply, "Why should we favor the comfort of men over the leadings of the Holy Spirit?"

He told me, "The Holy Spirit can work in 20 minutes or less." I explained to him my dilemma and that I felt the corporate gatherings of the body of Christ should be for boisterous praise and worship and for equipping the believers to go out from the church to do the work of ministry. He disagreed and said the vision for the church was no longer worship...that the new vision was to cater to those who did not know Jesus.

Without hesitation, I explained that my belief was that the vision of the church was not worship but that worship was part of the foundation of the church. His next question sent me reeling. "Do you feel like I am putting you out to pasture?"

I replied, "Not until you asked me that question...but I do now." He then came back to his point that worship was no longer the vision of the church. I expressed to him how I had been raised on a farm and never once did we go to the barn (the church) to get the harvest, but we were equipped at the barn and sent out into the fields to reap the harvest. I was adamant that he know how I felt about equipping the saints to go out into the fields to do the work of ministry, how I felt each home in our body should be considered a home church...a hospital for those who need Jesus. His next statement cut me to the core. "If you don't agree with the vision, you need to leave this church."

A few weeks later, my family quietly left this very special place of ministry we had called home for 10 years. I was allowed to make a resignation video in which I explained to the people that it had become very clear to me and to our family that our time at this church body had come to an end. Absolutely no animosity was expressed. I felt this would lessen the chances for division in the body. I grieve this loss to this day but know I am where God wants me. Melinda and I never missed a beat. We continue to minister out of our home and actually incorporated—became officially recognized by the state of Oklahoma—as All In All Church.

One more story worth mentioning, yet another very painful and fiery trial, was the making of the documentary of my life story called "Sing Over Me." Filmed in 2012 and 2013, I was so excited to have a world-class chronicle of my life and so excited to ask some of my famous Christian friends for a simple statement of endorsement for use in promotion of the film. One of the world's most renowned Bible teachers (someone you would readily recognize) and a friend of mine was the first person I approached to ask for an endorsement.

Their reply? "That's your calling, Dennis. Not mine." After that, I stopped asking for endorsements. Thousands and thousands of people have watched the video and I have heard from many of them about how God has used the film to minister to their lives, but I have a difficult time not focusing on the lack of endorsement by the Christian community.

I felt abandoned...alone...thrown under the bus...stranded in the middle of nowhere once again. But I can honestly say Father God has never once abandoned me...never once left me alone... never once thrown me under the bus. He is with me in the middle of nowhere.

8
WHEN DEATH COMES

"Every parting gives a foretaste of death, every reunion a hint of the resurrection."

— ARTHUR SCHOPENHAUER

"There's something about death that is comforting. The thought that you could die tomorrow frees you to appreciate your life now."

— ANGELINA JOLIE

"There is a sacredness in tears. They are not the mark of weakness, but of power. They speak more eloquently than ten thousand tongues. They are the messengers of overwhelming grief, of deep contrition, and of unspeakable love."

— WASHINGTON IRVING

Through the years, I have ministered to thousands who have been devastated by the loss of a loved one. Grief is the feeling of loss we experience when someone we love passes away. Mourning is the outward expression of that grief. God's Word says in Matthew 5:4, "Blessed are those who mourn, for they shall be comforted."

Forever etched in my memories is the passing away of my grandmother Jernigan when I was 14 years old. She was a spiritual mentor. She encouraged me to keep playing the piano even when I was bullied for doing so by schoolmates. She opened my eyes to some of the deeper places in the kingdom of God than I had the capacity to fully understand at that time. She often told me things the Holy Spirit would speak to her and encouraged me to watch Christian TV shows with her. We were so close that she entrusted me with her own funeral plans! The day after she went to be with the Lord, my dad and my grandmother's pastor were in the kitchen discussing funeral arrangements. When I realized what they were doing, I went and retrieved my grandmother's plans and brought them to that table and said, "These are the songs and passages of Scripture grandma wanted used for her service. She wanted it to be about Jesus and us and not about her. She wanted to bless us with these songs to help us mourn and these verses to bring us comfort."

At the funeral I was emotionally stoic. I wanted to appear strong. Somehow I managed to make it through without shedding a tear. When it came time for the family to get into the limousine to head to the graveside portion of her memorial, I was told there was only enough room for my parents and three brothers and that I would need to ride to the cemetery with another relative. Devastated that I did not get to ride with my family, feeling slighted and alone, I got into my relative's car and sobbed uncontrollably until we arrived at the gravesite some 20 miles away. In that 20-minute ride, I began to understand the cleansing power of mourning. Grief is something we hold inside. Mourning is the release of that grief.

In 1993, my ministry had expanded nationwide and I was in need of someone to handle all the ministry product sales (CDs, music books, and other materials) at my ministry venues. My dad, at age 55, was in a stage in his life where he could come to work for me. It was during that year that he and my mom began driving the product van across the nation. For the next 24 years, my parents worked for me in the ministry. In fact, my mom still does.

In the summer of 2017, my dad fell and could not get up several times. After weeks of these falling episodes, my mom called one day and told me dad had fallen and was unconscious and that she had called for an ambulance. My mom and dad still lived on the farm where we grew up, 16 miles away from where Melinda and I live. I raced to the farm in time to see them placing my father in the ambulance and will never forget that drive as I followed my ailing dad to the hospital in Muskogee. It brought back memories of following the family car so many years ago at my grandmother Jernigan's funeral. I cried all the way to the hospital.

After several weeks, it became obvious that my dad was not going to improve. He was moved from a regular hospital room and into the ICU, where he was intubated and could not speak. At one point, he motioned for me to come close so he could tell me something. "Do you need a drink, dad?" I asked. He shook his head back and forth in frustration. "Do you need me to call your nurse for you?" Again, he frustratedly shook his head. All this time, he kept motioning for whatever it was he needed and I kept giving him the wrong answers! I felt helpless as to what to do to understand my dad's need until my son, Ezra, walked in and said, "Hi, grandpa. It's me. Ezra."

I explained to Ezra that grandpa was frustrated because he was unable to speak and get whatever it was he needed. Ezra leaned over to his grandpa's face and asked, "What do you need, grandpa?" My dad motioned with his hands and got out an unintelligible (to me) whisper to which Ezra replied, "You need your bed raised up so you can see better, grandpa?" My dad finally nodded in complete satisfaction, "Yes!" Moments like that were like drops of mercy and grace on my soul and on the soul of our family that seemed to be God's simple presence saying, "I am going through this with you…and here is a bit of joy to help you along the way."

While dad was still in ICU, I was in the middle of writing a children's book about the time my dad and I grew a basketball goal from a seed. This story is one of my favorite memories of my dad from my childhood and is completely true. One of my favorite things to do is to tell this story in public gatherings because of the way it expresses the meaning of love. My fear was that my dad would not live to see it published. To alleviate that fear, I contacted my publisher, Bart Dahmer, of Innovo Publishing in Memphis and asked if there would be any way he could somehow get me a single copy to show my dad.

Three days later, a single book, complete with the final beautiful illustrations, arrived. While my mom watched, I took the book to my dad's bedside and showed him the cover. His eyes lit up. His demeanor changed. I asked him if he remembered growing that basketball goal with me. He nodded to the affirmative. We then went through the book page by page so my dad could see the beautiful artwork of our friend, Deb Grizzle. When we had looked through the entire book, I told my dad that this story, his sacrifice of love for me and our family, would live on for generations to come and that this was an awesome legacy to leave the generations of our family.

My brother Bob is a funeral director in Dallas. His wife is a nurse practitioner. My brother Sam's wife, Leslea, is a nurse at the local VA hospital. My niece, Chrysta, is also a nurse practitioner. So we had an abundance of help when it came to understanding what the doctors would tell us concerning my dad, explaining in laymen's terms what my dad was experiencing and what each medication was for and assuring us that he was not in pain. My brother Paul and his wife, Sandy, were like rocks in the family, always pointing us to Jesus. Paul told me he and dad had talked extensively about death and dying and that my dad was very prepared and very at peace with the possibility. He said dad had been insistent that we not bury him in a suit and tie so one day, while dad was still in ICU, Paul leaned over to my dad and whispered, "You know we're gonna bury you in a suit." We laugh about that to this day because we know dad loved hearing that. Yet one more moment of joy in the midst of sorrow.

Knowing his time was short, all the grandchildren came to say their goodbyes, except for our daughter, Hannah, who lives in Australia with her husband Ash and their girls, Elliott and Matilda. They had planned a trip to the U.S. for August so we knew the window of her seeing her grandpa again in this life was short. We decided to place a FaceTime call to Hannah so she could talk to her grandpa. She told him how much she loved him and then asked him the most wonderful question. "Grandpa, we're coming to see you in two weeks. Can you hold on until we can get there?" My dad nodded his affirmation.

Two weeks later, Hannah and her family arrived. By this time, we had placed dad in an extended care facility since my mom could not give him the end-of-life care he needed at home. Hannah and Ash took their girls in to see him and he was alert and whispering his responses as best he could. It was obvious he had been waiting for this moment…that he had held on until he could see all his grandchildren and great-grandchildren one last time.

During those last few days in the extended care facility, my three brothers and I took turns spending the night with my dad to give my mom a break. I would spend only one night there. My youngest brother, Sam, took the Wednesday night watch on August 30, 2017. At 5:30 a.m., I woke from a deep sleep with the urge to go to the hospital. I reasoned I was just experiencing fear and that everything was alright, so I nodded off to a drowsy sleep only to be awakened by Melinda saying, "Your brother Sam says you need to get to the care facility. Your dad just passed away!"

To this day, I regret not following what I now know was the calling of the Holy Spirit that morning. A middle-of-nowhere moment in a major middle-of-nowhere moment! The way I put that regret to rest was by asking the Lord for His perspective. His reply? "I wanted Sam to be with your dad. Your dad is with Me now and he is doing fine. It did not matter one way or the other if you had been there or not. He came with Me in peace and is no longer suffering."

One by one, my brothers and their families joined us at the facility. All but one of our nine children and their children were able to be there next to my dad's body as we comforted one another and reminisced about my dad's amazing life. (Asa, who had gotten to do a FaceTime call with his granddad, was stranded in New Zealand with visa issues.) The first thing that came to mind was how he had waited until he could see Hannah and her family before he finally let go. Their visit had taken place the day before he passed away. A drop of amazing grace and realization of God's presence in a middle-of-nowhere moment.

Later that day, my brother Paul handed me a piece of paper dad had given him on April 1, 2005. It read as follows:

LAST WILL & TESTAMENT OF SAMUEL ROBERT JERNIGAN

Of sound mind (I wonder sometimes) and sound body (wearing out)

FUNERAL ARRANGEMENTS

Do NOT (I repeat do NOT) put a suit and tie on me!!! If you do I'll come back and haunt ye!!!

READ PSALM 23

Take your pick of song, live or recorded. This is a celebration time!!

(Songs)
    In My Father's Life
    Take Me There
    Baptize Me
    My Yoke Is Easy
    I Trust In Thee
    Nobody Can Take My Life Away From Me
    The Rhythm of Life
    The Fruit of My Lips
    The Lord Is My Shepherd
    I Lift My Hands
    This Day
    We Win

It would be good if all the grandkids could sing something. You Are My All In All - The Sheep Song (I Am A Sheep) - It Was My Sin? I won't be there anyway so do what you want to.

All the grandkids can be pallbearers.

Having Bob handle all the funeral arrangements was amazing. We celebrated my dad's life. I told those in attendance that we were going to exalt and worship Jesus together and that my dad had selected 15 of my songs. After the audience exhaled, I explained that we would only share five and that I would share the rest on social media in the days to come! Worship was glorious and God was present. My son, Israel, read Psalm 23. The grandchildren sang I Am a Sheep. Paul delivered the eulogy and reminded everyone that dad was ready to die because he knew Whose he was and where he was headed. Sam preached the Gospel for at least 45 minutes (I may be exaggerating a bit here… but close!). My nephew, Caleb (who is a pastor and awesome worship leader), closed the service with a healing sermon of hope in Jesus Christ.

By the way, we did not bury dad in a suit and tie. We buried him in one of his cowboy shirts and a pair of jeans. After the service, I felt relief and release. Comfort and love. Peace and assurance that my dad was with Jesus. The only problem was that he was no longer here with us.

To be honest, I never expected to experience the level of grief I felt in the days following my dad's death. I began to experience panic attacks and found it more and more difficult to sleep. I went into a deep depression that only exacerbated the sorrow I was experiencing. Even though this was not a realistic expectation, I honestly thought my dad would be one of those people that would always be there. And now he wasn't. I did not know how to deal with it even though I was very adept at helping others work through their grief with mourning.

After a year of this deep darkness I had sunken into, my long-time mentor, Jack Taylor, became so concerned with my well-being that he flew me to Florida to spend a week with him. He literally spent seven days praying over me, pointing out lies I was believing, and helping me replace those lies with the truth of God's Word. I came away with a lifted heart and a new hope. I had finally come out of the middle of nowhere that had been brought on by the loss of my dad. But it did not take long for the next middle-of-nowhere moment to come to light.

9

PARKINSON'S

"We were promised sufferings. They were part of the program. We were even told, 'Blessed are they that mourn,' and I accept it. I've got nothing that I hadn't bargained for. Of course it is different when the thing happens to oneself, not to others, and in reality, not imagination."

— C.S. LEWIS, A GRIEF OBSERVED

In early August of 2018, almost one year after my dad's death, I was feeling somewhat back to normal with regard to my overall mental and emotional well-being, but I began to experience excruciating pain in my right knee. About four years before I had gone through surgery to replace my left knee. It did not take the orthopedic surgeon long to review my x-rays and explain my pain was due to all the cartilage worn away in my knee and that I would need to have the knee replaced.

During my first knee replacement, I had moments afterward in which the pain meds caused me to experience panic attacks.

With Melinda at my side in the hospital, I would tell her when my mind was being inundated with fear. All I said to her was, "Speak truth to me." She immediately began telling me all the good things that were true in my life. She went down the list, beginning with the fact that she was right there with me, that I had nine amazing children, that I had 11 awesome grandchildren, that God was right there with me, that I could declare the Word of God to my own soul. After only a few moments of her speaking truth to my mind, the panic attack would just be gone! For the year following my second knee replacement, we would have many such moments of me waking up in sheer panic and Melinda faithfully speaking truth to me and bringing calm to my soul.

For that reason, I dreaded the second knee surgery, but the physical pain became the driving force behind my decision to go through with it. Of course, the surgery was successful and after only a few weeks of therapy I was walking again, pain free, yet something just didn't seem right.

Although my physical pain had alleviated, my mind seemed to be in a fog. At first, I simply attributed it to the effects of the paint meds following my surgery. Several public ministry times happened, and I found myself physically and emotionally exhausted after these wonderful moments of corporate worship. Yet rather than feeling the usual euphoria I had always felt after such moments, I felt dread.

By November of 2018, it became a strain to sing. At times, my voice just was not there. Raspy and hoarse replaced what was formally clear and pleasing. Again, I assumed it was due to the intubation required during my knee surgery and that my voice would return with time. It never returned. After experiencing an ENT threading a tube with a camera on the end through my nose, I was able to see that one of my vocal folds had a deep indentation in it, like the indentation a surgical intubation might cause. The

ENT told me it might take up to 18 months for this type of trauma to heal. Losing my voice was one of the most heart-wrenching middle-of-nowhere moments I have ever experienced. My mistake was in believing that my voice was part of my identity. Reality was that God was about to take me on an incredible journey that makes all the persecution I have ever experienced feel like a walk in the park.

During the final months of 2018, I continued to battle an ever-deepening mental fog. At times, I could form words in my mind but could not get my mouth to speak those words. It became difficult to walk without feeling I was in slow motion. To be honest, I thought that this must be how a zombie feels! My self-awareness of these issues and natural introverted personality made me not want to be around people at all.

It was also during those fall months of 2018 that we began to notice a slight tremor in my right hand, specifically the three right-most fingers. Once again, I went to see my orthopedic surgeon, assuming the tremors were caused by nerve damage I possibly suffered during a rotator cuff surgery three years before. After a nerve test on my arm, which honestly felt like electroshock torture, my surgeon told me there was damage but none sufficient enough to cause the tremors. He suggested I schedule an appointment with a neurosurgeon. When I asked why, he matter-of-factly said, "It is my opinion that you are experiencing the onset of Parkinson's disease."

My heart sank and my mind went into full-on denial mode. My brain continued to deteriorate into hours of foggy wilderness. My tremors began to increase. My speech became plodding and slurred and I sank into major depression. I began to lose weight. People began to notice my delayed response times in conversation. Christmas of 2018 became one of the most painful periods of my life.

While at an annual family reunion in December, I felt so self-conscious around people that I spent the majority of that reunion walking around outside with my youngest grandchildren. While I LOVE being with my grandchildren, I dreaded the now-normal questions from family and friends in whom I had no doubt about their love for me. "Are you okay, Dennis?" and What's wrong with you, DJ?"

Even though we had received the initial diagnosis of Parkinson's, we needed to have that officially confirmed by a neurologist. Trying to get an appointment with a specialist was a major undertaking. In November of 2018, we were referred to a neurologist but were not able to get an appointment until January 28, 2019! I continued to suffer and go downhill. By the time of my appointment, I had lost more than 40 pounds and my brain had sunken into a continual fog, making conversation and ministry next to impossible for me. I had absolutely no stamina.

Finally, January 28, 2019, came. After looking at my charts and MRI results, the doctor simply said, "You have Parkinson's." I felt like I had just been handed a death sentence, yet I felt a weird kind of relief from the constant state of mental denial I had been trying to sustain over the past few months. Bottom line: They do not really understand what causes Parkinson's. For some reason, the brain stops producing dopamine. Dopamine is a neurotransmitter, which is associated with reward-motivated behavior. In simple terms, it is a feel-good hormone that floods one's brain when something good is experienced.

The doctor said I could live another 30 years and people might not even notice I had the disease. He immediately prescribed daily doses of dopamine and told me that if my depression and tremors lessened, I had Parkinson's. Of course, Melinda and I got the prescription filled ASAP and I took my first dose that afternoon. My mood lifted and my tremors lessened. Middle-of-nowhere moment. I had Parkinson's disease.

Melinda and I immediately decided we would honor the

remaining concert and ministry events for the coming year but would take no new engagements in order to allow my mind to heal. We also felt we needed to be honest with our family and friends and with those to whom we ministered. Truth sets us free. The first step of truth is honesty. While I believe that was the right thing to do, I was not prepared for what was to follow.

Both Melinda and I began to be inundated with "cures" for Parkinson's. The sheer number of remedies suggested by well-meaning people was overwhelming. If I had tried to implement everything suggested, I would not have had enough time in the day to get to each one!

One of the most difficult things for me to endure even a year and a half down the road from the initial diagnosis is the way people respond to me when I tell them I have Parkinson's. I understand people love me and that they want what is best for me, but sometimes it feels like I have just told them the world has ended and that I am on death's bed. Here are a few examples of what people have said to me that did not bring me much comfort.

"Oh, Dennis! I'm so sorry!"

"Oh, man! How terrible!"

And my favorite, "We're so sorry for what you are about to go through. We recently lost a parent to Parkinson's and what you are facing is absolutely horrible."

Long story short, rather than allowing Parkinson's to define me, Melinda and I decided to see it from the King's point of view. It is our view that this is not a sickness unto death but a sickness unto God's glory. Our goal? How can we use Parkinson's for the kingdom of God? God wastes nothing. I find my relevance and purpose in my relationship with Him and not in the failing of my physical body! My plan is to find God in the middle-of-nowhere of Parkinson's!

Even before the confirmation of the diagnosis, Melinda and I began to make plans for how we would face this head-on. We are determined to live this life in an abundant way, giving God thanks in the midst of the storm for the opportunity to experience an ever-deepening outpouring of grace and intimacy with Him.

Practically, we have recognized the need of discipline in my life as a means of continuing to renew my mind. The truth is still the truth regardless of my physical or mental state! One of the best things to do when dealing with Parkinson's is to exercise. I swim 14 laps a day, Monday through Friday.

My weekly schedule is set in stone, yet open to spontaneous altering as needed. On Mondays, I write scripts for podcasts and post short videos on social media. On Tuesdays, I record podcasts and post them for listeners. On Wednesdays, I write and post a week's worth of daily devotions for my Patreon team members. On Wednesday evenings, I lead worship, teach and minister in our home. We incorporated our home as All In All Church, and we minister to a small group in our home each week. On Thursdays, I write whatever the Lord brings to mind, whether music or fiction or whatever. On Fridays, I simply devote to being creative in some way.

As of this writing, my depression has lifted. My stamina has increased. I feel direction and purpose. I daily think of ways to minister to my family and am very conscious of leaving as huge a spiritual legacy for my children and grandchildren and generations to come as possible.

Sleeplessness is a side effect of Parkinson's so falling asleep can be quite the battle, even with sleep meds. Being around people still makes me battle feelings of being overwhelmed, but I force myself into being with people in spite of my feelings. I know I need people even though it would be easier to avoid them.

Just as I did with same-sex attraction, I am doing with Parkinson's. I am renewing my mind daily by putting off the lies of the enemy and replacing them with the truth of God's Word. I am reorienting myself to God's truth in the midst of this battle. Being told I have Parkinson's was like being trapped in a wave on a beach, that wave tossing me and turning me so violently that I couldn't tell up from down. To reorient myself, I simply need to stand up on Solid Ground. Jesus is here as my Solid Rock even in Parkinson's. He is still with me. He has not moved. He has not changed. His love for me absolutely refutes and casts down fear.

We were not promised an easy life or that we would not have to suffer, but we were promised we would be given grace to endure and that we would never be left alone. Why Parkinson's? Why me? Why not Parkinson's? Why not me? Many have suffered far worse life-altering things than I have, but I have a great cloud of witnesses I can look to for encouragement when the enemy's lies would have me give up rather than fight the good fight of faith.

Noah built an ark and saved humanity even while others mocked him for doing so.

Moses led the children of Israel out of bondage and to the promised land even though he never got to set foot there.

David defeated Goliath even when his own people doubted his ability. David committed murder and adultery, yet he is known to this day as being a man after God's own heart.

Stephen was stoned for his faith.

Paul was imprisoned and executed for the sake of the Gospel.

And Jesus...

Need I say more?

> Therefore, since we have so great a cloud of witnesses surrounding us, let us also lay aside every encumbrance and the sin which so easily entangles us, and let us run with endurance the race that is set before us, fixing our eyes on Jesus, the

author and perfecter of faith, who for the joy set before Him endured the cross, despising the shame, and has sat down at the right hand of the throne of God.

— HEBREWS 12:1-2

10

MELINDA'S POINT OF VIEW

"Like airplane passengers, let's not forget to put on our own oxygen masks first ... we are no good to our loved ones if we collapse under the strain."

— SUBMITTED BY PETER BAILEY ON CARINGBRIDGE.ORG

"No act of kindness, no matter how small, is ever wasted."

— AESOP

The following is Melinda's perspective on how Parkinson's affected her. What I realized as I read her account was that I had allowed Parkinson's to make me very self-focused. My feelings of aloneness kept me from seeing my need to minister to my wife. It made me realize that I had been fighting for me...and not for us...not for her. My eyes were opened to the way the disease affected her and I felt she needed to share her middle-of-nowhere moment with you. Whether the one suffering the disease or the one taking care of the one with the diagnosis, both parties suffer. We are a team. We are one. Reading her account made me renounce my self-focus and helped me renew the fight from a different point of view. Rather than fighting for myself, I became determined to fight for her, for our children, for our grandchildren and for the generations to come. Here is Melinda's heart:

When I found out Dennis had Parkinson's, I was actually relieved we had a diagnosis that made sense for the symptoms he had been experiencing for a long time.

Looking back, I believe there were many triggers that led to this. He had several surgeries and was put on opioids for pain. They opened up a part of his brain that caused panic attacks and made it hard for him to break through and control his thoughts. The panic attacks continued and amplified with another knee replacement surgery, then the subsequent damage to his vocal cords, which was totally devastating.

We had so many questions. What would we do for income? How would we continue to minister? Would we have energy for our grandkids? How could I help him? What would my role look like now? Could I bear more of the responsibility? Would we have to sell our forever home? He was my strength and now I could see times where he was slipping away. I was starting to crumble.

Another trauma was the death of his father. Dennis was the firstborn and yet had grown up not ever feeling quite enough for his dad. Those pains had been healed through the years, and those last days in the hospital, sitting and comforting his dad and mom as he watched his father struggle and go in and out of reality, was the emotional tipping point. At night, his panic attacks would be triggered by memories of his dad dying in the hospital and thoughts that he couldn't breathe. We had many sleepless nights where prayers, speaking truths, and reading scriptures were helping, and we were getting through it, but barely. It became such a battlefield. There were times I was so panicked and worried he was going to have another panic attack that I couldn't sleep, and we didn't really leave the house.

Our ministry and concert schedule was pulled back to almost nothing because he could barely sing. Travel, and being around a lot of people, exhausted him. We could not attend family functions; he would need to leave almost as soon as we got there because he would start to panic. It was overwhelming and just too much. Just the thought of having people around him put him in a state of panic. I could not sleep because he couldn't sleep. We were a mess.

Our doctor was so kind and patient with us both—praying with us, crying with us, grieving with us. He said to me, "You are experiencing compassion fatigue." I felt so relieved that someone actually put words to what I was experiencing, that he understood and knew what I was going through. We knew how to overcome the enemy, but this was different. We knew how to take our thoughts captive, put on God's word and speak truth to every situation, which we did frequently. One of our daughters even created Dennis a Truth Jar filled with inspiring scriptures, fun family jokes, and memories written on strips of paper for Dennis to pull out and read or remember when he would have these times of panic. These "truths" would work for a season, but, again, this was different.

Dennis had lost a lot of weight. He had a blank stare on his face most of the time, which was not like him at all. His sense of smell was gone. People around us every day started to notice and wondered what was wrong. The kids noticed. He was fearful the grandkids would notice, and so he pulled away from everyone even more. When we found out it was Parkinson's, it all made sense.

The tremors started after the knee replacement surgery, but a year before that, he had had extensive surgery on his shoulder to repair a torn rotator cuff. I had thought maybe the tremors were from nerve damage or scar tissue built up from that surgery, which would have explained the tingling and small tremors. Tests were run and, yes, he had nerve damage, but they were sure it was not from the surgery, which left us puzzled. I was still not convinced the nerves and scar tissue didn't have a part to play in the issues he was having. He lost the use of three of his fingers on his dominant right hand, which made it very difficult to play the piano or do any physical tasks that demanded full grip-strength. It was so hard to see my husband having to adapt and not be able to do some of the tasks he used to easily do. At times I felt afraid; it was like I was holding my breath, not knowing what would happen next, but I remained strong and had a pretty positive attitude throughout the entire process. I assured him that I did not care that his hand shook or that his arm got weak. He still had a hand. I reminded him, and still do, that I did not marry him because of his hands. That was not who he was.

"We are in this together. We are a team." This was a statement we proclaimed repeatedly throughout this entire process, aloud, during times of fear and doubt, which helped keep our minds focused on what was right and true. When we finally were able to get the tests done, which seemed like forever to us since it takes such a long time to get in to see a neurologist and receive a diagnosis, we finally felt heard. We felt hopeful. We actually had a bit of relief from our unknown thoughts and fears and at least knew we could develop a plan of how to help him. With the series of medication the doctor prescribed, we saw immediate results and improvement from the tremors, in his countenance, and general well-being. This was good for me, and I could let go of my breath a bit.

Dennis was like his old self—smiling again, laughing, engaging with family and friends, and creating again. His voice returned over time, but the damage was done.

The medications are tricky. Keeping a strict schedule, exercise, and reducing stress has helped. We work together to save his energy for our grandchildren and family, our closest friends and home church, which is crucial to our well-being. I need to be with people, and time with the grandchildren, family, and friends is also energizing for Dennis.

We made many adjustments during this time of navigating the new discovery of Parkinson's in our lives. This disease does not only affect the person that has it, but the caregiver and those around them as well. I am very much an extrovert naturally—loving our house full of people, enjoying going out and talking to people, trying new things, just being social and being with people. During this downward spiral before the actual diagnosis, and since, I have found myself becoming an introvert, and I hate it. Now, don't misunderstand me. I don't hate introverts; I am married to one and have a family full of them, whom I love dearly. I understand their special gift and its place in this world and would not wish to change them at all, but I need to be with people to be my best self. I need to engage with them, I need to get out and about, go places, shop, and talk, as well as do things with friends. But I have found myself becoming content at home by my husband's side, wanting to be with him just in case he needs me if he has a panic attack, to make sure he is not overdoing it, that he has his snack and remembers to take his meds at the right times, which he does. I just feel the need to watch over him. And then the COVID-19 shutdown happened, which has made things much worse for people like me.

We had planned for over a year to have a huge family reunion in our home with all of our children and grandchildren. It was going to be the first time we would have all been together in six years. Our children live all over the U.S. and in Australia. My mother and her husband, who is 84, were going to fly in as well, thinking it could be the last chance to see our kids and grandkids from Australia. It was a big deal. Then, boom, everything shut down. We were all devastated, but it was out of our control. It was not a happy time. Many tears were shed.

I love our family and miss my kids and grandkids so much. This is still very hard to write about. My heart longed for all of us to be together, for the grandchildren to all play together, for Dennis and I to get to listen to stories and good memories from each of our children growing up, and for all the children to get to see their dad and grandparents. I find myself not wanting the time to slip away. Not knowing how this disease will progress is the hardest part. The thought of our children and grandchildren not being able to have a relationship with their dad/grandfather and know how amazing he is, his strength of character, his sense of humor and ability to tell a joke, the creative way he crafts a story, the way he leads in worship, his compassion for the hurting...this is why I treasure those times together. It grieved me so when this was taken away. Knowing that it hurts him as well, and he saves every bit of energy he has for his family, makes me love him even more.

In our relationship, we have both worked hard at championing each other in whatever we are doing. I found myself taking on a more protective role, trying to anticipate situations that would trigger stress or panic, and helping avoid or prepare the best I could so that Dennis would be able to handle them easily. The hard part is not coming across like a mother hovering over a child. Dennis is a grown man, but I can discern when Parkinson's shuts him down or he is getting tired and needs to leave so he doesn't overdo it and regret it later. This is a hard dance to learn the steps to. I feel like I have to lead at times. There have been moments of personal breakdowns where I had just become completely undone, a mess, and had hard and uncomfortable discussions with Dennis through my sobs and tears, trying to explain and get the right words out to help him understand my needs. And he has shared openly with me how he feels. Dennis is patient, kind, and listens well, and for that I am grateful.

A good day is when we both have had sleep. Sleep is the biggest and most difficult issue we are dealing with at the moment. When we are both rested and he can maintain his swimming and work schedule, then we both have a good day. I work on my jewelry orders and have time to be creative as well as taking care of any household chores. Dennis will get us lunch and rest a bit, then go back to work a bit more. We watch Jeopardy together. I cook dinner, and we will play with grandkids if they come over or watch some of our TV shows together in the evening. While watching TV, I might work in my chair on my social media or finish up creating any jewelry project I need to finish. We just like being with each other. My very favorite days are Wednesdays. That is the day I schedule grocery pickup, any errands I need to do, or shopping that needs to be done. Basically, I just get out of the house. My need to engage with people and visit is why this is one of my favorite days. That has been hard since the COVID-19 shutdown.

A few weeks ago, some of the restrictions were lifted, and Dennis suggested I get out of the house. He could see that I was needing social interaction. I went into every shop I could. I talked to everyone waiting in line to get into shops, six feet away, at the checkout through Plexiglas screens, at the drive-thru picking up my lunch—all while still social distancing—and had such a great day. My spirits were lifted, and I came home so happy. I came through our door a new person. It's so important for my well-being. Just engaging with others and getting out brought me so much joy. Seeing other people was life.

Dennis is not much of a talker. This is one of the hardest parts for me since I have a lot of words I need to say. Because of his Parkinson's, he has become more isolated and much more of an introvert than he already was. That, combined with the COVID-

19 quarantine, made for days where, if I am totally honest, I lost it. I lost myself. Yes, at times I feel so alone in this journey.

I know that is not completely true. We have hundreds of supporters and a large group of family and friends who love us dearly, would do anything for us, and are there for us. This season for me is just different. Many days, I am completely worn out from always pointing out the positive, saying encouraging words, lifting up Dennis by trying to serve him, juggling everyday things on my own, not wanting to burden him with too much because it would overwhelm him, finding the right moments to share difficult decisions or needs that may come up, and not knowing if he will be able to handle, fully comprehend or even be able to respond. I know it's the Parkinson's and not me, and it's okay, but the challenge is real.

This part is difficult to write. Dennis is so kind and caring and a good listener, and there are many times I have told him, "I need you to be the strong one so I can be weak." Does that make sense? There are times I wish he would decide and not ask me, or wish he would just reach out and grab me for a passionate embrace. I miss the times he would plan dates for us. There are days I wonder, "Who is going to take care of me?" Knowing that I can share these things with him helps, and I am so grateful to have him as a partner and a friend. He is the one I chose and I am so grateful he allows me to be honest with him, but my struggle to share with him is still not easy for me. I feel insecure and inadequate in my ability to express how I feel in words. It's hard to say things in a way where he truly understands, without him feeling hurt or attacked. It's hard to share with a man who is so gifted, an elegant writer, who is sensitive and full of mercy, and who writes songs and amazing stories for a living. I do not always feel like I have the right words to say how I feel. At times I feel misunderstood, so I just hold my thoughts and feelings in. The Lord knows my heart, but the enemy tries to use my insecurities to divide us.

Even as I type this, tears are flowing, but I pray my honesty will help others to be honest in their journey.

There are bad days when neither of us have slept well, or we have had a full weekend—a few days of company or daily events. Many days I don't think I have spoken a complete sentence to him, or when I do, I get no response to my comments. We sit together in silence. I am grateful he is at least sitting with me, but those are not good days for me.

What do I do when I need emotional care? Well, I have a number of things. Creativity comes easily for me, and I love diving into projects and figuring out how to make do with what I already have. Besides making jewelry, I love sewing, gardening and doing projects for our home. I have always been able to find an item and see what I could make out of it.

The grandchildren are my biggest source of joy, and they bring life to our home. Spending time with them is vital to my emotional well-being. I try to go to lunch with friends when I can, but I feel a sense of responsibility to do as much as I can to bring in income, so I find it harder to get away from home since it interrupts the creative process. I need to do better at taking the time to be with friends and tending to my own well-being.

One of the highlights of my week is our home church, which meets in our living room. We worship together and pray for each other. Dennis and I both love these times and it really does energize us. Our home has always been a safe place, a refuge, a hospital for the broken. Now it is our safe place.

I find that I am at peace at home, now that our children have grown and are out of the house. Dennis and I have both traveled the world and have ministered in some amazing places, but we love coming home. It is our refuge, where we can breathe, our place where we feel safe and most relaxed. My goal is to create a comfortable atmosphere where we can enjoy our family and share our lives. Dennis and I have both had many times of brokenness in our lives—physically, spiritually, and mentally—and the journey with Parkinson's is just one more chance for us, together, to receive from the Lord the grace we need to heal and walk through whatever may lie ahead.

I am part of a private Facebook support group for caregivers of Parkinson's. Many well-meaning friends and supporters have sent us research and articles, and we are grateful, but they are very overwhelming to Dennis, so I am the one who does most of the reading, research and education, which can be a never-ending mountain to climb. Dwelling on the "what ifs" is not helpful to either of us. I am not saying we have not prepared ourselves for the future. We have a POA, living will, trust, as well as my name on all of our accounts, and I have access to all of his passwords and accounts. I have learned what my future might look like with the Parkinson's, but each person is different, and this is a disease full of unknowns, very different for everyone.

What is known is that my hope is in the Lord. Everyday Dennis and I both trust that He will get us through this with the grace He alone can provide. The Lord promises to give me wings to fly and strength to endure and finish this race. Dennis and I are a team. The Lord knew we needed each other. Dennis is strong when I am weak, and I can be strong for him in his time of need. We are fighting this together with the Lord's help, one day at a time.

Our children are such a blessing. Each one steps in to help across the oceans and miles. WhatsApp and FaceTime are our lifelines and we communicate daily. Living in this age of technology has been a huge blessing and keeps us laughing and connected during difficult days. Our kids encourage and support both their dad and me with their own unique giftings.

I have learned and been reminded at this point of our journey that the Lord is, and always has been, faithful. He has always provided for every need. He has always healed in His time. When we have grown weary, He always has been a source of strength, through our friends and family, songs of worship, and the truths of His Word. He never fails.

I have learned that, as a caregiver, it is so important to not lose who you are. If you are naturally an extrovert, like myself, it is vital to find ways to engage with people and spend time with friends and family. As soon as things open up after COVID-19, we will be visiting grandchildren and planning our family reunion again. It is essential to remember to laugh and bring joy to your home and situation, and helps to shift the mindset to what is truth. That is my goal though all of this. I chose to see the good and to dwell on the positive. We are truly blessed and grateful. We will finish this race strong. We are a team with strength in numbers. We know who wrote the Book and how it ends! We win!

Since reading her chapter, I have made a concerted effort to be more aware of her needs. We have re-instituted a weekly date night. I am taking advantage of her need for passionate embraces and we are enjoying the pleasures of being one. I am working on my listening skills and fighting through the foggy times to do so. She is my reason to fight on…and I want her to know she is worth fighting for. I love you, Melinda, and am the most blessed man on earth because of you.

11
THE MIDDLE OF NOWHERE

"Pray that your loneliness may spur you into finding something to live for, great enough to die for."

— DAG HAMMARSKJOLD

The Middle of Nowhere
Words & Music: Dennis Jernigan
March 3, 2017

Where can I go from Your presence?
Where can I go from Your grace?
How wounded and how broken must my heart be before
Your healing can't reach that place?
In the middle of nowhere!
In the middle of nowhere!
Where can I go when forgotten?
Where can I go when alone?
How long before my blinded eyes are able to see
This world is not my home?

THE MIDDLE OF NOWHERE

In the middle of nowhere!
In the middle of nowhere!

In the middle of suff'ring!
In the middle of sorrow!
In the middle of pain!
In the middle of heartache!
In the middle of a desert!
In the middle of a driving rain!
Oh, Father, meet me there!
Father, meet me there!
In the middle of nowhere!
In the middle of nowhere!

In the middle of empty!
In the middle of the wilderness!
In the middle alone!
In the middle of the fire!
In the middle of darkness!
Middle of far from home!
Oh, Father, meet me there!
Father, meet me there!
In the middle of nowhere!
In the middle of nowhere!
In the middle of nowhere!
Father, meet me there!

Nothing I go through is wasted
When seen from the King's point of view!
My life a grand adventure where I'm never alone
And when I get there I find You!
In the middle of nowhere!
In the middle of nowhere!

In the middle of grateful!
In the middle of deliverance!
In the middle of joy!
In the middle of triumph!
The middle of the enemy!
In the middle of a lie destroyed!
Oh, Father, meet me there!
Father, meet me there!
In the middle of anywhere!
In the middle of anywhere!

In the middle of a healing!
In the middle of life!
In the middle of grace!
In the middle of a miracle!
In the middle of freedom!
In the middle of a King's embrace!
Oh, Father, meet me there!
Father, meet me there!
In the middle of anywhere!
In the middle of anywhere!

In 2017, I was asked to minister in the town of Hartley, Texas, at Hartley Christian Fellowship. As people asked the question, "Where is Hartley?" I explained to them it was located about 78 miles north of Amarillo. Their response? That's the middle of nowhere!

As was my custom, I asked the pastor if there was any specific need he wanted me to address as I ministered to his congregation. He wrote me back with, "I pray for renewed passion and an openness and love for our changing community culturally. A return to our first love as followers of Christ."

Taking this to heart, I began to ask the Lord if there were any things He would have me specifically address in relation to what the pastor had written. All I could hear in my thoughts was the phrase "in the middle of nowhere." I could not shake that thought, and knowing how the Lord operates in my mind, I prepared to receive a song about being stuck in the middle of nowhere.

The more I pondered that phrase, the more definitions I came up with as to what it means to be in the middle of nowhere. According to the Cambridge Dictionary, the phrase means "far away from any towns and cities and where few people live." Hartley certainly fit that definition, but I knew the meaning would have deeper spiritual ramifications, so I kept meditating on the phrase and a song was born. Following are some of the thoughts that emerged.

The middle of nowhere could mean being lost in the wilderness. Just as the children of Israel wandered around in a physical wilderness, their wilderness was also one of a spiritual nature. Although they did not always correlate the two, the spiritual was actually more important than the physical. The physical wilderness was provided to show the people of God their spiritual condition.

They had just spent the past 400 years in the wilderness of slavery to Egypt and now they found themselves free from that bondage. It did not take long for attitudes of gratitude to change to second thoughts and grumbling against leadership. In the very midst of the wilderness of the Sinai, God Himself had led them by a cloud in the daylight and by a pillar of fire by night. He had parted the Red Sea. And on a more personal level for each family and individual, He provided food fresh each morning in the form of manna. Yet, they chose to see the wilderness rather than the love and presence and power of God being demonstrated in their midst!

How often do we gaze upon our circumstances, surmising we are in the wilderness, smack dab in the middle of nowhere, yet neglect to see the love and presence and power of God being demonstrated in our life daily?

Being in the middle of nowhere can be as simple as feeling alone. In that respect, being in the middle of nowhere can mean feeling alone in the middle of a crowd. The middle of nowhere can be in the middle of millions of people in New York City for the Macy's Thanksgiving Day Parade and feeling as if no one can even see you.

The good news is that we cannot possibly ever be alone if we remind ourselves that the God we are in relationship with is anywhere we happen to be. Being alone with God is not a bad place to be. In fact, I—being an introvert aside—find being alone with God rather invigorating. To be with God in intimacy…Him seeing all of me and loving me anyway and me taking the time to gaze into His presence…is to recharge my batteries on every level. Jesus intentionally went into the middle of nowhere for this very reason: To be alone with His Father and to recharge his spiritual, emotional, mental, and physical batteries. In other words, being in the middle of nowhere can be a very good thing.

When we are willing to stand alone for our faith, when we are willing to speak truth to those we love, when we risk loving through service, we face the risk of being misunderstood. Because of the nature of my own story—freedom from homosexual identity and now knowing I am heterosexual—I often feel as if I live in the middle of nowhere, in the middle of being misunderstood. The fact is that if we pursue Jesus with the passion with which He pursued us, we will be misunderstood. Each of the apostles had to walk through the wilderness of being misunderstood. They preached love. The world heard hate. The world, thanks to the deception of the enemy, is walking in darkness apart from Christ. The most loving thing to tell someone is that they need a Savior because of their sin. No one wants to be told they are wrong about anything, yet that was one of the most loving things ever spoken to me. "Dennis, you are in sin."

Just like Stephen who was stoned to death for his faith in Christ, we may be misunderstood to the degree that our very lives are threatened. Just as with the children of Israel who had the choice of seeing and experiencing God's love, presence, and power, Stephen chose to see from the Lord's point of view while in the middle of nowhere. While being stoned to death for preaching the truth of Jesus, He chose to look into the heavenly places.

> "But being full of the Holy Spirit, he gazed intently into heaven and saw the glory of God, and Jesus standing at the right hand of God; and he said, 'Behold, I see the heavens opened up and the Son of Man standing at the right hand of God.'"
>
> — ACTS 7:55-56

The stoning continued but so did the faith of Stephen. "They went on stoning Stephen as he called on the Lord and said, 'Lord Jesus, receive my spirit!'"

— ACTS 7:59

When finding ourselves in the middle of nowhere, whether in a desert, in a crowd, or being stoned, we must realize that even there we are not alone. Could it be that finding one's self in the middle of nowhere is a good — and grand — thing? It all depends on the point of view, I suppose.

We can see a cloud of obscurity, or we can see a cloud that guides.

We can see a fiery trial or we can see a fiery pillar of God's protection.

We can see a sea raging all around us with no way through, or we can see a parting of that very sea.

We can see eking out a bare existence, or we can see even the smallest morsel as manna from heaven.

We can see emptiness, or we can see the opportunity to be filled.

We can see brokenness or the opportunity to be poured out.

We can see a desert, or we can see a chance to meet with our Maker in the oasis of His love for us.

We can see wounding, or we can offer our hearts and hurts to the Healer.

We can see the middle of nowhere, or we can see the love, presence, and power of our God.

Ultimately, the middle of nowhere is a good and grand place because it is there that we meet the God who meets all our needs!

12

I'VE BEEN THROUGH FIRE

"Tribulation will not hurt you, unless as it too often does; it hardens you and makes you sour, narrow and skeptical."

— EDWIN HUBBELL CHAPIN

I've Been Through Fire
Words & Music: Dennis Jernigan
July 3, 2014

I've been through fire
Hot enough to make a grown man
Want to lay down and die
I've been through fire hot enough
To burn away everything
Leaving just a semblance of life
I've been through fire
Hot enough to make me feel
I have no place to call home
I've been through fire but I tell you,

Been through fire, been through Hell
But I have never been alone

Through the fire You have brought me!
Through the fire I have never been alone!
Through the fire You have sought me
In a fashion all Your own
With a passion hot enough to melt a heart of stone!

I've been through fire
Hot enough to make me wonder
Where I'd find that next breath
I've been through fire so consuming
Like I had someone there grooming me
For imminent death
I've been through fire
Where the fury of the flame
Left my heart harder than stone
I've been through fire but I tell you,
Been through fire, been through Hell
But I have never been alone

Through the fire You have brought me!
Through the fire I have never been alone!
Through the fire You have sought me
In a fashion all Your own
With a passion hot enough to melt a heart of stone!

Lord, Your love is like a fire!
The flames keep growing higher to consume me!
Lord, Your love is like a fire!
Your love is my desire!
So consume me!

Burning fire fueled by passion
Where Your love, like waves, comes crashin'
To consume me!
Burning fire fueled by passion,
Make my heart like You in fashion
And consume me!

Through the fire You have brought me!
Through the fire I have never been alone!
Through the fire You have sought me
In a fashion all Your own
With a passion hot enough to melt a heart of stone!

I've been through fire
Hot enough to make a grown man
Want to lay down and die
I've been through fire

Here is what I wrote concerning the initial writing of this song. Since its writing, the fires of my life have only seemed to multiply and grow more intense.

> Sometimes I feel I will be completely consumed by them, but then I remember how much my God loves me. For each and every fire I have had to endure, what is not of the Lord has been burned away, leaving only what is purely of the Lord standing. As I am able to look back now and see each incident from the Lord's point of view, I don't see the ashes of loss. I see the richness and abundance of the treasures of my life…and have come out shining like gold.
>
> Yes, I have been persecuted. Yes, I have been dealt the loss of my voice. Yes, I have been diagnosed with Parkinson's disease. Yes, I have been betrayed by friends. Yes, I have been

guilty of believing the lies of the enemy from time to time. Yes, I have been wounded beyond what I ever thought I could bear. But I do not see the ashes of my life. I see a faithful, loving, beautiful wife of 37 years (as of this writing). I see nine amazing children, six amazing sons and daughters-in-law. I see (so far) 11 mind-blowingly awesome grandchildren who infuse my life with exquisite joy. I see thousands of songs born out of the trials of my life that are now sung around the world. What has taken the place of the ashes of my life is a long legacy of testimony to the power and love of our amazing God.

I have had to endure a lot of fire through the years simply based on my leaving the homosexual way of thinking—my OLD identity—by virtue of my relationship with Jesus Christ. Many people seem happy for me. Many seem appalled. Many seem fearful to take a stand one way or the other. I just want those who desire such freedom to know it is possible through Jesus Christ. Because of a documentary that is about to be released detailing my story ("Sing Over Me"), I fully expect the fire to intensify. In my own strength I am not ready, but by God's grace, I will be in the moment. Just as He was in the midst of the fire with Shadrach, Meshach, and Abednego, I know He will be with me. Incidentally, I prefer to hear this song sung from the Father's perspective toward me.

As I have already detailed in previous chapters, I have experienced persecution—fiery trials—on many occasions. What has kept me going in such middle-of-nowhere moments is the understanding that I have never gone through one single fiery trial alone. Shadrach, Meshach and Abednego were cast into a furnace as punishment for not bowing to and worshiping the Babylonian king, Nebuchadnezzar. Three were cast into that unsurvivable oven, but four were seen walking about in the flames unscathed!

But these three men, Shadrach, Meshach and Abednego, were

thrown into fell into the midst of the furnace of blazing fire still tied up. Then Nebuchadnezzar the king was astounded and stood up in haste; he said to his high officials, "Was it not three men we cast bound into the midst of the fire?" They replied to the king, "Certainly, O king." He said, "Look! I see four men loosed and walking about in the midst of the fire without harm, and the appearance of the fourth is like a son of the gods!'" Daniel 3:23-25

Shadrach, Meshach and Abednego were not alone. The Lord was with them IN the furnace, going through the fire WITH them. He is the same God that walks with us through the fires of our lives! Death by fire is painful. Being burned causes some of the deepest and most excruciating pain any human can encounter. Fires leave scars. Fires burn things away, leaving ashen ruins. I have experienced deep excruciating mental and emotional pain to such a degree I wished I had died, but God has always been there to bring comfort. I have been scarred by the fires of this life, but I have chosen to see these scars as the evidence of God's grace. A scar simply means I have gone through something painful but serves as evidence of the healing power of God. My scars say to the world, "Yes, I have been through fire. I have the scars to prove it, but look what God has done!"

Within the short biblical account of Shadrach, Meshach and Abednego I used, one phrase speaks volumes to the fiery trials of life. King Nebuchadnezzar said, "Look! I see four men loosed and walking about in the midst of the fire without harm!" The key phrase there? "I see four men LOOSED!" Those three men cast into the fire simply for standing alone for God Almighty had been cast into it BOUND! Fire is painful, but fire has a way of burning away the things that bind us.

Since the release of *Sing Over Me*, I have received many vile comments and have been mocked and scorned and reviled as if I were Satan incarnate, but all those momentary experiences of pain are soothed by the balm of God's grace with each person who tells me they have seen the film and that God has used it to change their lives forever. God has taken the ashes of my life and made something beautiful of them. This is the legacy and story behind the song "I've Been Through Fire."

> The Spirit of the Lord God is upon Me,
>   Because the Lord has anointed Me
>   To preach good tidings to the poor;
>   He has sent Me to heal the brokenhearted,
>   To proclaim liberty to the captives,
>   And the opening of the prison to those who are bound;
>   To proclaim the acceptable year of the Lord,
>   And the day of vengeance of our God;
>   To comfort all who mourn,
>   To console those who mourn in Zion,
>   To give them beauty for ashes,
>   The oil of joy for mourning,
>   The garment of praise for the spirit of heaviness;
>   That they may be called trees of righteousness,
>   The planting of the Lord, that He may be glorified.
>
> — ISAIAH 61:1-3

Go back and read the lyrics of this song from the Lord's point of view. You might just see and hear Jesus…

13
STEAL AWAY

"Look, if I were alone in the world, I would have the right to choose despair, solitude and self-fulfillment. But I am not alone."

— ELIE WIESEL

"Give yourself a gift of five minutes of contemplation in awe of everything you see around you. Go outside and turn your attention to the many miracles around you. This five-minute-a-day regimen of appreciation and gratitude will help you to focus your life in awe."

— WAYNE DYER

Steal Away
Words & Music: Dennis Jernigan
January 28, 2013

If I could steal away

And ride the wings of the wind
If I could steal away
Just every now and then
That would be sweet
That would be wonderful
That would be overwhelming joy to me!
If I could steal away
Into a most secret place
If I could steal away
Be gone without a trace
That would be sweet
That would be wonderful
That would be overwhelming joy to me!

In Your presence
I can steal away!
In Your presence!
Any time, night or day!
Where You conquer any mountain
Where You calm the raging sea
Where You wrap Your arms around me
Though imprisoned, I am free!
In Your presence
I can steal away!
In Your presence!
Any time, night or day!
I can steal away!
I can steal away with You!

If I could steal away
And get away for just awhile
If I could steal away

In awestruck wonder like a child
That would be sweet
That would be wonderful
That would be overwhelming joy to me!
If I could steal away
Condensing hours to one breath
If I could steal away
And no one even know I'd left.
That would be sweet
That would be wonderful
That would be overwhelming joy to me!

In Your presence
I can steal away!
In Your presence!
Any time, night or day!
Where You conquer any mountain
Where You calm the raging sea
Where You wrap Your arms around me
Though imprisoned, I am free!
In Your presence
I can steal away!
In Your presence!
Any time, night or day!
I can steal away!
I can steal away with You!

If I could steal away
And ride the wings of the wind
If I could steal away
Just every now and then
That would be sweet

That would be wonderful
That would be overwhelming joy to me!

If I could steal away...

So many times in my life I have been confronted with a painful situation and wished I could run away and hide. When I was a boy struggling with same-sex attraction, I wanted to be invisible. When I was called names and bullied, I wanted to be anywhere but in those moments. What do I do to steal away when Parkinson's consumes me? What do I do to steal away when my once strong voice has been reduced to a whimper? More times than I care to admit, I wished God could just suspend time and let me time travel to a place of future safety, but our God is the God of yesterday, today, and tomorrow. He transcends time, stepping in and out of it as He sees fit. He has even been known to stop time!

I've been thinking a lot lately about God's ability to suspend time. In Joshua's day, He caused the universe to stand still. Has anything changed in His ability to do so? I began asking Him to take the small portions of the day when I have brief times to spend with Him and multiply His presence. In other words, in a five-minute window of time, refresh and restore as if I had just spent hours in rest or asleep. He is faithful to meet with us in our daily rush and hectic schedules. This song is meant to be a catalyst to help us get away from it all even when we can't physically do so!

> Then Joshua spoke to the Lord in the day when the Lord delivered up the Amorites before the sons of Israel, and he said in the sight of Israel,
> "O sun, stand still at Gibeon,
> And O moon in the valley of Aijalon."

> So the sun stood still, and the moon stopped,
> Until the nation avenged themselves of their enemies.

Is it not written in the book of Jashar? And the sun stopped in the middle of the sky and did not hasten to go down for about a whole day. There was no day like that before it or after it, when the Lord listened to the voice of a man; for the Lord fought for Israel.

— JOSHUA 10:12-14

God can meet with us in the middle of nowhere: In an overwhelming storm, a fiery furnace, financial ruin, unbearable pain, unfathomable sorrow, the bombardment of the enemy's lies, the most seductive temptation, in a loud and boisterous crowd, in the middle of feeling utterly and irrevocably alone.

Alone in my Parkinson's? No. God is there with comfort and love.

Alone in the grief of my diagnosis? No. God is there, mourning with me, comforting with His presence.

Alone in my suffering? No. God is there, sharing and bearing the burden with me, giving grace along the way.

Alone in the slow degradation and fading of my mind into the fogginess of Parkinson's? No. God is holding my hand through the fog, urging me to follow Him and bathing me with the mind of Christ.

My point? With God, time is irrelevant. He is with us in the middle of any circumstance we could possibly imagine, and He can take even a few seconds of our human awareness of time and multiply those few seconds into a day's worth of rest and refreshment. Just as God caused time to stand still for the children of Israel when faced with the onslaught of their sworn enemy, He can do the same for us. The Deliverer—the God of Israel—is the same Deliverer and God with us. After all, He is Immanuel—God with us.

> To everything there is a season,
>> A time for every purpose under heaven…
>
>> — ECCLESIASTES 3:1 NKJV

14

DANCE WITH ME, MY KING

"Intimacy is not a happy medium. It is a way of being in which the tension between distance and closeness is dissolved and a new horizon appears. Intimacy is beyond fear."

— HENRI NOUWEN

"All the ills of mankind, all the tragic misfortunes that fill the history books, all the political blunders, all the failures of the great leaders have arisen merely from a lack of skill at dancing."

— MOLIERE

Dance With Me, My King
Words & Music: Dennis Jernigan
September 28, 1987

Dance with me, my King
While the heavens sing

I love Your name
How I love Your holy name
Dance with me, my King
While the heavens sing
I love Your name
How I love Your holy name

I love Your name
Jesus, how I love Your holy, holy name
I love Your name
Exalt Your name
Most high
I love Your name
Exalt Your name
Most high
Dance with me
Dance with me
Dance with me, my King

This is an old song from the days when I first began leading worship in a public setting in Oklahoma City. God had been doing so many wonderful things in my life, and I was being drawn more and more into the healing places one finds in an intimate relationship with Christ. Though I was still not publicly sharing my story of deliverance, I was still very honest and open with the Lord about my past. I discovered that as I openly confessed my sins and hurts to the Lord I was not rejected but rather I found a depth of embrace I never thought possible before.

    The thing I feared most was being found out and then being rejected because of my shortcomings. What I found was just the opposite. This song was a song of intimacy I would sing privately to the Lord. When I began to release it publicly, ladies would be drawn to dance beautiful dances of worship to the Lord and many would be ministered to. Even though I could not share the depths from which the song had come concerning my past, I did find great joy in seeing others experience the same release and freedom one finds in an intimate dance with the Savior. And now you finally know the rest of the story!

As I deal with Parkinson's and the loss of my voice, I have grown accustomed to and I expect intimacy with the Lord. It is the key to my sanity and key to my comfort. Intimacy with God alleviates pain and despoils fear. Intimacy occurs when I turn to my God and say, "Here is my heart, Father. Into me see," hiding nothing from Him and withholding nothing of myself from Him. That is but the first step of intimacy with God, though. True intimacy occurs when I turn my heart to Him in naked honesty and He turns His heart toward me in that same moment and says to me, "Here is My heart, son. Into Me see." In that moment, true intimacy is attained. Nothing hidden. Everything shared.

I will never forget the first time I danced with my wife, face to face. I will never forget the intimacy of that moment. I will never forget the physical intimacy of our union on our wedding night. Why? Because is was the first time, as a man, I felt completely known and accepted by another human being. It was also the first time I felt I knew another human being—my wife—in such a way that can only be described as pure holy ecstasy.

Knowing God is like that. He knows everything about me and loves me anyway! My greatest desire and the deepest desire of my human heart is to know and to be known by my Maker. It is this type of "nothing hiddenness" that I felt when writing this song. Completely known. Knowing another completely.

I dance with my King for the sheer joy of the way He has transformed my sorrow into song…

You have turned for me my mourning into dancing;

> You have loosed my sackcloth and girded me with gladness…
>
> — PSALM 30:11

I dance with my King for the sheer massive worth of who He is…

> Let them praise His name with dancing;
> Let them sing praises to Him with timbrel and lyre.
>
> — PSALM 149:3

I dance with my King for the cleansing He brought to my sin-stained soul…

> "Then the virgin will rejoice in the dance,
> And the young men and the old, together,
> For I will turn their mourning into joy
> And will comfort them and give them joy for their sorrow."
>
> — JEREMIAH 31:13

I dance with my King for loving me even when I turned my back on Him…for loving me right where I was…for loving me enough to not leave me there…

> And the son said to him, "Father, I have sinned against heaven and in your sight; I am no longer worthy to be called your son." But the father said to his slaves, "Quickly bring out the best robe and put it on him, and put a ring on his hand and sandals on his feet; and bring the fattened calf, kill it, and let us eat and celebrate; for this son of mine was dead and has come to life

again; he was lost and has been found." And they began to celebrate.

— LUKE 15:21-24

I dance with my King as a child with a Father...just because...

15

I AM UNDONE

"Everyone is broken; every mortal man or woman is broken in some way, shape, or form."

— MATT HARDY

"This perfection is the restoration of man to the state of holiness from which he fell, by creating him anew in Christ Jesus, and restoring to him that image and likeness of God which he has lost."

— ADAM CLARKE

I Am Undone
Words & Music: Dennis Jernigan
March 13, 2013

You took my broken heart
Once cast aside like trash is
You made my heart brand new

Brought beauty from the ashes
And here I stand in awe
Of perfect love and power
Here I stand in awe
Of my God!

I am undone by Your mercy
I am undone by Your grace
I am undone by Your goodness
And Your sure, strong embrace
I am undone by Your dying
I am undone by such love
I am undone by Your sacrifice
Who could love me that much?
I am undone
I am undone

You took a wasted life
And made that life worth living
You filled my heart with joy
Reduced me to thanksgiving
And here I stand in awe
Of perfect love and power
Here I stand in awe
Of my God!

I am undone by Your mercy
I am undone by Your grace
I am undone by Your goodness
And Your sure, strong embrace
I am undone by Your dying
I am undone by such love
I am undone by Your sacrifice

Who could love me that much?
I am undone
I am undone

The world would have me labeled a bigot, a hater, a fool for daring to say someone might leave behind a homosexual identity in exchange for a heterosexual identity. The old me was undone. The new me is in a constant state of ripping away the grave clothes. I am still being undone and still being reborn and rebuilt. I am undone emotionally and in every way by His deeply passionate love for me.

This year this song was born, 2013, was like a whirlwind. Not only was I going to be a grandfather, but a film crew would be making a documentary of my life in the hopes of obtaining major theatrical release. In addition and in conjunction with the movie, I was writing my life story in a way and to such a deep level I was left feeling naked and exposed, but in a holy and cleansing and healing way.

As I think about all these things, I am overwhelmed at God's redeeming love in my life. As *Sing Over Me* is now available on Amazon Prime and the book of the same title is also available, I am more convinced than ever of God's plan and purpose for my life, and more convinced than ever of His deep, abiding love for me. Yes, I was once emotionally undone by my sin yet bound in a tangle of lies and deceit, but God's love leaves me even more emotionally undone yet stable and on solid ground, all while he undoes/unravels the mess sin had made of my life. This song was born in the midst of all these happenings and, once you hear it, you will understand the awe and wonder I feel at the revelation of God's love in my life. That is my prayer for you as well—that you would see, feel and experience God's deep abiding love for you here and now.

Being undone by God's love requires trust. Following after

Jesus in a dark world requires trust. Running the race of life with a sense of purpose and destiny requires trust. Going through middle-of-nowhere moments when it is difficult to feel loved, to see the Light, to believe your purpose, and to know God wastes nothing in the entire process of life requires trust. When I am undone, I fall apart. The best place I have found to fall apart is in the arms of Jesus. To be undone by His love is to be restored in the deepest, darkest recesses of the soul.

Yes, I am physically, emotionally, and mentally undone by Parkinson's, but I am learning to allow that "undone-ness" to teach me how to glory in and even boast in my weakness that He might be strong in me. God has been so faithful throughout the course of my life to pick up the broken pieces of my existence and put them back together. He has restored my soul countless times. What He has been faithful to do in the past, He is faithful to do in the here and now. My diagnosis did not surprise God or catch Him off guard. He is still the same loving, redeeming God who wastes nothing, whose love for me is a promise from His Word to me. How does Parkinson's change or affect His restorative love for me? It doesn't! I am, once again, undone and once again, Father has met me there. He is using Parkinson's for His kingdom and for His glory and for my good. I trust Him. Period.

> So will My word be which goes forth from My mouth;
>> It will not return to Me empty,
>> Without accomplishing what I desire,
>> And without succeeding in the matter for which I sent it.
>
> — ISAIAH 55:11

16

FATHER, SING OVER ME

"I can't talk about my singing. I'm inside it. How can you describe something you're inside of?"

— JANIS JOPLIN

You are my hiding place;
    You preserve me from trouble;
    You surround me with songs of deliverance. Selah.

— PSALM 32:7

Father, Sing Over Me
Words & Music: Dennis Jernigan
March 27, 2018

You are Living Water in a dry and weary land
In the shaking times, You're Solid Rock where I can stand
When the storms of life come, You're a Shelter over me

You are Light in darkness Watching over me
In the times of wounding You come healing me
When fear would come surrounding
You come singing over me

Father, sing over me when I'm losing it!
Father, sing over me when I'm wounded!
Father, sing over me with Your presence!
Father, sing over me with Your love!
Father, sing over me love unending!
Father, sing over me! I'm surrendering!
Father, sing over me with Your presence!
Father, sing over me!
Father, sing over me!
Father, sing over me!

I will be your Righteousness and you be My redeemed!
I will be your Holiness and I have washed you clean!
Child, hear Me singing!
This is what I'm singing over you!

I will be your Hiding Place! My love concealing you!
I will be your comfort! Let My love come healing through!
Child, hear Me singing! This is what I'm singing
  over you!

I will be Provider! I will meet your every need!
I will be your Champion! Find in Me your victory!
Child, hear Me singing! This is what I'm singing over
  you!

I will be right with you! I will never, ever leave!
I will be your Shepherd! If you let Me, I will lead!

Child, hear Me singing! This is what I'm singing over

Father, sing over me when I'm losing it!
Father, sing over me when I'm wounded!
Father, sing over me with Your presence!
Father, sing over me with Your love!
Father, sing over me love unending!
Father, sing over me! I'm surrendering!
Father, sing over me with Your presence!
Father, sing over me!
Father, sing over me!
Father, sing over me!

Since my dad passed away in August of 2017, I have had a very difficult time. Just being real here. After he passed away, I had several good weeks where I felt tinges of grief and felt I was traversing the journey pretty well and then the first week of December hit and I began to experience panic attacks and many sleepless nights. Grief was overwhelming me and I had not expected it to be so overwhelming. My first Christmas without my dad caught me by surprise, as did his December birthday.

Grief is the feeling of loss. Mourning is the outward expression of that loss and I was not doing so well at mourning. I got some relief as time passed by, but when March came around in 2018, I began to fall back down into the bottomless pit grief can become. Melinda had been fighting for me and holding me up emotionally, but she became overwhelmed by my emotional overload.

She began experiencing compassion fatigue. She had come to the end of her ability to hold me up along with her own emotional needs. She told me she could not do it anymore and that I needed to begin fighting for myself, to fight harder at digging myself out of the deep dark pit of emotional self-pity. I needed to hear that.

This song was my way of fighting out of the darkness and what I have been challenging people to do for decades. I needed to practice what I preached! This has become my new go-to song of deliverance. It also helps me to focus on the needs of others rather than on always having to focus on my own. My needs are met when I seek to meet the needs of others.

Concerning grief and mourning as it relates to the diagnosis of Parkinson's disease, I had gone far too long without understanding that part of what I was experiencing was grief over my diagnosis. A friend just asked me one day, "Have you ever grieved the diagnosis of Parkinson's?" Those words hit me like a ton of bricks.

What I realized is that I had been holding that grief deeply inside of me in order to appear strong for my family. When I realized that this buildup of sorrow was doing more damage than good, I began to pour out my grief in active, outward mourning. I let go of the sorrow I felt at the loss of my physical stamina, the loss of my youth, the loss of my mental stamina, the potential loss of my life, the loss of time with children and grandchildren, the way my lack of mourning my diagnosis had robbed me of deeper intimacy with my wife. This song helps me mourn and move on from sorrow and into joy because God praised comfort to all those who mourn.

God's Word is true. He surrounds me with songs of deliverance. I just need to listen. He rejoices over me with singing. I just need to listen. When my Father sings over me, I am instantly aware of His presence completely consuming me…completely consuming my sorrow, my suffering, my pain, my worry, my fear, and my anxiety because He sings from the place of perfect, all-consuming love. The result of His singing? Grace to get through pain and deliverance from sorrow. What is left when grace and love intersect with a song from God's heart? Peace and joy. Dare to believe God sings over you.

This song is dedicated to Melinda. Thanks for fighting for me and for fighting the enemy with me. I love you.

Blessed are those who mourn, for they shall be comforted.

— MATTHEW 5:4

You are my hiding place;
  You preserve me from trouble;
  You surround me with songs of deliverance.
  Selah.

— PSALM 32:7

Here is my own translation of one of my favorite verses from God's Word:

The eternal self-existent God, the God Who is three in one; He Who dwells in the center of your being is a powerful and valiant warrior. He has come to set you free, to keep you safe, and to bring you victory. He is cheered and He beams with exceeding joy and takes pleasure in your presence. He has engraved a place for Himself in you and there He quietly rests in His love and affection for you. He cannot contain Himself at the thought of you and with the greatest of joy spins around wildly in anticipation over you…and has placed you above all other creations and in the highest place in His priorities. In fact, He shouts and sings in triumph, joyfully proclaiming the gladness of His heart in a song of rejoicing! All because of you!

— ZEPHANIAH 3:17

17

YOUR NAME IS BEAUTIFUL

"However weak we are, however poor, however little our faith, or however small our grace may be, our names are still written on His heart; nor shall we lose our share in Jesus' love."

— CHARLES SPURGEON

Your Name Is Beautiful
Words & Music: Dennis Jernigan
Words: July 6, 1987
Music: August 8, 1987

If there never was a song
For my feeble tongue to raise
If there nevermore was music
I would find a way to praise Your name
Your beautiful name
If there never was a body
Or a fleshly hand to raise
If I could not dance before You

I would find a way to praise Your name
Your beautiful name

With every fiber of my being
And every breath within my soul
Every thought I'd cast before You
Just to somehow let You know
I'd find a way to praise Your name

Your name is Beautiful
Your name is Peace
Your name is Mighty God
Your name is Prince of Peace
Your name is Wonderful
Your name is Holy One
Your name is Jesus
Jesus, Your name is beautiful to me

If I never knew Your healing
If my days were filled with pain
Just the fact that You are near me
Gives me strength to still proclaim
Your name
Your beautiful name
If I lost all my possessions
Or the family I hold dear
I would gladly give my life up
If it meant the world would hear Your name
Your beautiful name

With every fiber of my being
And every breath within my soul
Every thought I'd cast before You

Just to somehow let You know
I'd find a way to praise Your name

Your name is Beautiful
Your name is Peace
Your name is Mighty God
Your name is Prince of Peace

Your name is Wonderful
Your name is Holy One
Your name is Jesus
Jesus, Your name is beautiful to me

Following are the words I wrote about this song, "Your Name Is Beautiful," when I first received it way back in 1987:

> I was once challenged by someone who really questioned the need for outward expression of worship. This person asked me, "What if I were physically unable to express my worship? What if I could not lift my hands or dance before Him? How can I expect someone to do that?"
>
> My response? If we are talking about me, I am physically able to do so, so I WILL praise Him with my physical being, but let's say I was unable to move my limbs. What would I do then? The answer would still be the same. I'd still praise Him for all He has done for me! I'd blink my eyes in worship! I would dance in my mind! I would breathe as loudly as I could breathe to express in one way or another what Jesus Christ means to me!
>
> When we think about redemption and salvation, we need to see ourselves as being rendered able to move in our spirits... though once crippled and incapacitated by sin. When we are washed clean and redeemed of that sin, we are healed of our

weakness. Abiding in Jesus is learning to walk with Him. Worship is really like our spiritual therapy! Because I see how desperate my life was without Him, I would do anything He asked me to do in worship. I would be glad to do it. Because of that gratefulness in my life, I will use whatever gifting He has given me...whatever means I have available to give Him the glory He deserves. This song came as a result of these types of questions in my life. If I could not praise Him physically, I would find a way. Think about it. What would you do?

Since I wrote those words in 1987, the lyrics of this song have become both bittersweet and poignant, powerful and prophetic. In the song, questions are raised about whether or not I would praise God if I lost my ability to move or sing or praise my God with reckless abandon. Since my diagnosis with Parkinson's, these words are sweeter and more meaningful than ever to me and bring much comfort to my soul:

> *If there never was a song*
> *For my feeble tongue to raise*
> *If there nevermore was music*
> *I would find a way to praise Your name*
> *Your beautiful name*
>
> *If there never was a body*
> *Or a fleshly hand to raise*
> *If I could not dance before You*
> *I would find a way to praise Your name*
> *Your beautiful name*

With the diagnosis of Parkinson's, my world came crashing down in many ways. I lost my ability to sing as I once did. My body just doesn't seem to be healing as I would hope. I find it difficult to get some notes out regardless of how much I try. Most days, I experience pain and suffering in a physical and mental sense, yet I still make a daily choice to praise the name of Jesus. As of this writing, we are in the midst of the COVID-19 pandemic that is sweeping the world in 2020, leaving us feeling isolated and giving us moments of anxiousness as to whether we will be able to survive financially due to my illness. Even though the words of this song were written over 30 years ago, they ring more true than ever in my life.

If I never knew Your healing
If my days were filled with pain
Just the fact that You are near me
Gives me strength to still proclaim
Your name
Your beautiful name

If I lost all my possessions
Or the family I hold dear
I would gladly give my life up
If it meant the world would hear Your name
Your beautiful name

It is in the names of God that I find much solace from the world falling apart around me…comfort through the suffering of my disease. He is my Righteousness. He is my Holiness. He is my Healer. He is God With Us. He is my Shepherd. He is my Provider. He is my Peace. He is my Victory. He is Jesus. In that one name we find all that God is and so much more. The way we develop intimacy with someone is often by simply learning the other person's name. As I have learned the names God calls Himself, I have learned about His character and nature. In the process, I have come to understand the meaning of my own name as a child of God. Dennis means "worshipper." That is who I am, and I am known intimately by the One who gave me my name. There is great peace in knowing God knows my name and great comfort in expressing how I feel about all His name means to me.

Beautiful…

> The name of the Lord is a strong tower;
> The righteous runs into it and is safe.
>
> — PROVERBS 18:10

18
AT YOUR FEET

"In a position of utter desolation, when man cannot express himself in positive action, when his only achievement may consist in enduring his sufferings in the right way - an honorable way - in such a position man can, through loving contemplation of the image he carries of his beloved, achieve fulfillment."

— VIKTOR E. FRANKL

"Many people are alive but don't touch the miracle of being alive."

— THICH NHAT HANH

At Your Feet
Words & Music: Dennis Jernigan
April 5, 2018

I just need to sit at Your feet
It would be enough

To just feel You breathe on me

I just need to sit at Your feet
Just to know You're near
Would meet every single need

I just need to sit at Your feet
Knowing You still love me
Though You see right through me

I just need to sit at Your feet
Living Water! Bread of Life!
Just taking in long and deep!

Just to know I'm known
Just to know I'm loved
Just to sit here in Your presence is enough for me
At Your feet

Just to know You're here
Just to know I'm free
Free to sit here in Your presence
Simply be - just be
At Your feet

Holy! Holy!
I bow down before Your feet and
I cry holy!

Holy! Holy!
I bow down before Your feet and
I cry holy!

Holy! Holy!
I bow down before Your feet and
I cry holy!

Holy! Holy!
I bow down before Your feet and
I cry holy!

Just to know I'm known
Just to know I'm loved
Just to sit here in Your presence is enough for me
At Your feet

Just to know You're here
Just to know I'm free
Free to sit here in Your presence
Simply be - just be
At Your feet

The year 2018 was a rough one for me. Still grieving the loss of my dad, feeling mentally exhausted (not understanding at the time that what I was experiencing was, in fact, the onset of Parkinson's), and quite honestly, depressed, I found it difficult to see light at the end of the tunnel on most days. Along with these feelings came feelings of inadequacy, feelings of irrelevance, and wondering whether I was even needed. I felt that the best thing for me to do to take my mind off these things was to dive into my work more. I came up with a rigorous daily schedule for creativity that I thought would alleviate all those feelings. I was doing all I knew to do to combat the feelings of depression and the mental fogginess. What I was actually doing was pushing my emotions further inside my mind so as to not have to deal with them, but life has a way of forcing us to deal with the things we think we hide.

Since 1988, I had been sharing my story and music publicly and had never lacked for opportunities to share, receiving invitations to minister all over the U.S. and even the world. During 2018, I began to receive fewer and fewer invitations to minister. At first, Melinda and I came to a place of believing this was God trying to tell me to rest for a season, which was true. After all, I had knee replacement surgery coming up in August and I would need at least a couple of months to allow for recuperation and healing, but in my mind, I was still focused on the need to be doing something about my situation rather than simply being in the moment. The more I tried to perform my way through life, the weaker and more depressed I became. Then the Lord intervened.

A friend from my college days, whom I had not spoken with in almost 37 years, called me out of the blue one day and began to speak truth in love to my soul. His expression of faith was so bold and so unexpected that all I could do was listen and cry. He spoke things that I had not spoken to anyone else. He was very specific as he told me the Lord had shown him my depression and sorrow, and my mind was blown when he told me the Lord had spoken to him a word for me. That word? That I should sit at the feet of Jesus and just "be."

For years before Jesus found me, I had performed my way through life as a means of earning the acceptance and approval of others. When I was transformed in 1981, everything changed. I began the most incredible journey of my life that year. That journey was an epic saga of me learning to simply be God's son. That journey took me from the place of performing for His acceptance to the place of performing *because* I was accepted. I had preached that and lived that belief for years, but as we humans often do, we don't always realize there may be many layers of our former identities that we need to allow the Lord to peel away from us. This was one of those times.

One of the most difficult things I have ever learned, and continue to learn, is to simply be. To have this brother speak the words "sit at the feet of Jesus and just be" was like being hit in the face with a bucket of cold water on a hot summer's day. Those words began to work deeply in my soul. They reminded me that, like Lazarus, I had come out of the grave of sin and shame wrapped in the grave clothes of my former way of thinking. They reminded me that the journey was not over and that I still had believed many lies of the enemy concerning my need for acceptance and approval.

Hearing those words, it was as if my soul had been asleep and suddenly shocked into an awakening to and an awareness of my need to stop thinking negative thoughts about myself and my circumstances and to begin replacing those thoughts with the truth of God's Word. God's truth was still truth whether I was depressed or not! I suddenly realized I had slowly been falling back into a mindset of feeling I must perform to be accepted... that I must work hard and often to be considered a good man.

That day, I repented of my self-pity and wrote the words and music to the song "At Your Feet" as my first step in simply being God's son again without the need to perform for His love or acceptance. I began by expressing that God's presence was enough for me. My mind was consumed with a simple picture of me as a child, sitting at the feet of my Father while He simply spoke words of comfort and peace and acceptance and approval and affirmation and love. All this child had to do was to simply believe and receive that love.

In the moment this song was born, it was as if my feelings of being stranded in the middle of nowhere had been suddenly invaded by the love of God, and the result of that realization was that the middle of nowhere had suddenly become "the middle of now here." To "be" in God's presence is to believe He is with me regardless of my circumstances. Regardless of my inability to fully understand all my physical and mental weaknesses. Regardless of my pain. Regardless of my sorrow. The simple truth of understanding I was not alone and had NEVER been alone gave me permission to be weak in order to allow Him to be strong.

I believe the art of learning to *be* takes a lifetime, and then some, to fully comprehend and experience. It is coming to the place of utter helplessness and need as it intersects with God's presence that helps us get to the place of just *being*. It leaves one feeling naked and vulnerable. This is intimacy.

The greatest need of the human heart is to know and to be known. That need is only fully met in an intimate relationship with our Maker through faith in Jesus Christ. God loves me right where I am, but loves me enough to not leave me there. I am free to be who He calls me to be. I cease from my striving and simply know God. I have no doubt this will be my reality for the rest of my days on this earth and well into eternity as I seek to learn to simply be with my Father.

As a father of nine awesome children, I love them each just because they exist. As the grandfather of 11 (so far), I love them each simply because they exist. If I, as an earthly father, love to that degree, how much more does our heavenly Father love us just because we exist? Let's practice existing—just being—with Him and practice enjoying His presence through the journey of life.

I urge you, regardless of your circumstances, to incorporate the truths found in this song into the relationship you have with God. It is the process of renewing one's mind through right thinking. It is the way we learn the art of simply being. Take time each day just to *be*. That's my goal from here on out.

19
OUR GOD

"God will use whatever he wants to display his glory. Heavens and stars. History and nations. People and problems."

— MAX LUCADO

"A man can no more diminish God's glory by refusing to worship Him than a lunatic can put out the sun by scribbling the word 'darkness' on the walls of his cell."

— C. S. LEWIS

Our God
Words & Music: Dennis Jernigan
January 15, 2015

Our God is holy
Our God is great in mercy
Our God is holy
Great and greatly to be praised

Our God is holy
Our God is great in mercy
Our God is holy
Great and greatly to be praised

I praise You with all my might
I will praise You only
I praise You with all my life
You alone are holy

Holy! Holy!
Holy God Almighty!
Holy! Holy!
Holy is the Lord our God!

Our God is the awesome God
Who reigns in power and love
Our God is the awesome God
Who gave His Son redeeming us

Our God is the only God Who heals
Any broken heart He seals
The repentant heart with
Precious blood He shed for us
Our God!

One of the best things I have done in my relationship with God through the years has been to learn about His nature, His character, what makes Him…Him. The simple and most practical way I have done this is to learn what He calls Himself. Why is that important? Who He is tells us who we are because we are His children, and children tend to take on the traits passed through their genes from their parents! Since I am God's son, His spiritual

DNA flows through my spiritual veins and informs me in my identity.

Another simple and practical way I have come to understand the nature of God and to uncover and release more of His spiritual DNA into my own spiritual veins is the act of worship and praise. As I worship God in song, He lavishes His love on me as He surrounds me with songs of deliverance. This song, "Our God," came about as I simply practiced what I preached. Worshiping God is tangible expression of relationship with my Maker and reduces my thoughts to those of naked and utter intimacy. He sees me and loves me, no matter what.

Knowing who God says He is gives me guidance when I need to reorient myself and my thoughts from that of the world. Knowing who God says He is gives me a solid place to anchor my thoughts. Knowing who God says He is invigorates my relationship with Him. Think of it this way: One of the first steps in beginning any relationship is to find out the other person's name.

My wife's name—Melinda—means "beautiful." When I met her, I could not take my eyes off her because she was, indeed, very physically beautiful. As of this writing, we have known one another for 42 years and have been married for 37. I know her on a physical level, a mental level, an emotional level, and on a spiritual level. On every one of those levels, I find great beauty. One would think that after so many years of knowing another person, they would come to the end of discovering new facets of that relationship and that person. This is fascinating to me. When I hear her name, I subconsciously and instantly associate her name with beauty and strength and remember, for the umpteenth time, that I have only touched the tip of the iceberg in my understanding of who she is!

That is how my relationship with God is. The more I discover of His nature, the more mystery I encounter! As in the mystery of knowing my wife, the mystery of who God is always leads to deeper and unexplored places in my relationship with Him. Who God is speaks volumes to my soul when I find myself in a middle-of-nowhere situation.

When I was born again, I found it difficult to think of myself as clean before the Lord due to my sin and depraved way of thinking. God revealed Himself in the name "I Am Your Holiness - I AM Your Sanctification" (Jehovah Mekoddishkem). As I began to put off the old ways of thinking—the constant guilt and shame—and began to replace them with the new, I found myself feeling pure and unashamed…and holy…like my Father. He has set me apart for Himself, and that reality causes me to set myself apart for Him.

When I began my spiritual quest to know God and to be known by Him, I often found myself reverting to my old ways of thinking in regard to my self-inflicted need to perform for God's love and acceptance and approval. God then revealed Himself in the name "I Am Your Righteousness" (Jehovah Tsidkenu). When I understood that Jesus Christ had paid the debt I owed for my sin and left me in right standing with God, the spiritual DNA of this truth came flooding through my spiritual veins: I am the righteousness of God through faith in Jesus Christ!

In times of feeling confused, scattered and floundering my way through the middle of nowhere, I have come to rely upon the name of God, "I Am Your Shepherd" (Jehovah-Raah). He leads me through the valley of the shadow of death called Parkinson's. He watches over me through the long, sleepless nights, surrounding me with songs of deliverance and security. He provides Living Water and Bread of Life. He literally restores my soul. He astounds me with His mercy during the occasional lapses of taking my eyes off Him. He binds up my wounds and calls me to follow Him. He invites me to sit at the very table of the feast of His presence even when surrounded by the sometimes crippling lies and temptations of the enemy. His DNA runs through my soul and gives me the desire and grace to extend the same comfort to those around me.

He calls Himself "I Am Your Banner of Victory" (Jehovah Nissi). Quite simply, I have read the end of The Book and understand fully that, no matter what, I win! When I came to the place of understanding that His victorious DNA flows through my spiritual veins, I began to experience great strides in victory over the former temptations and former thoughts that formerly led me to self-focus and self-destruction. Through this knowledge of God, I came to the place of denouncing my former identity as a victim and began to view myself as a victor…as more than a conqueror!

As I have walked out the journey of life with my God, I have had many moments and opportunities to discover the fullness of the name "I Am Your Provider" (Jehovah Jireh). When Melinda and I were first married, we were dirt poor. We survived some weeks on popcorn and potatoes. When those resources became unaffordable, we simply stepped out in bold faith and asked the Lord to provide for our needs. On more than one occasion, we found a bag of groceries at our front door. When we were considering selling our wedding rings to pay the rent and buy groceries, God, through the people of our church family, gave us a car, showered us with baby gifts, and gave us $3,000! I could write a book, telling story after story of Him living up to His name as Provider. His providing nature flows through my veins as I feel compelled to provide for the physical, mental, emotional, and spiritual needs of others.

He reveals Himself in the name "I Am Your Peace" (Jehovah Shalom). Over the many twists and turns of my life's journey, I have encountered spiritual warfare, temptation, persecution, storms, fiery trials, physical pain and suffering, and deep and intense sorrow. In each of these segments of my journey, He has been there with me, whispering "peace, be still" to the storms of my mind, singing songs of love that dispel and eradicate the fear in the dark times, speaking words of wisdom from which to anchor my scattered thoughts. In His presence, I find peace. I am like my Father. I enjoy His presence because I know He enjoys mine.

Father God calls Himself Jehovah Shammah, meaning "I Am Here." When we understand that we never leave God's presence, we have a constant anchor and a constant lifeline…a constant Companion and Friend. I believe we either forget God is with us or we simply choose to ignore His presence. But God does not ignore my presence even when I ignore His! This does my soul a world of good as it relates to Parkinson's. One of the symptoms I am experiencing is a feeling of not being present in certain moments. I feel mentally invisible. I sometimes feel trapped in my mind, screaming to those I am trying to communicate with and nothing's coming out of my mouth. During such moments, I am driven to the anchor of my soul that says, "I'm right here, son. I Am right here." I know He is faithful to be with me because I simply love being with my children and grandchildren. And if just being with them brings such peace and joy to my mind, how much more does our heavenly Father enjoy just being with us.

God refers to Himself by a myriad of names. Redeemer. Lord God of Hosts. Savior. Lion of the Tribe of Judah. Lamb of God. Holy Spirit. Jesus. Jehovah. King of Kings. Lord of Lords. I could go on and on, but I'll end this chapter and the story of this song, "Our God," with one of my favorite names of God. He calls Himself Jehovah Rapha, which means, "I Am Your Healer." Has God healed me of Parkinson's yet? No. Will He? One way or another! He healed me of my past. He restored the years the devouring locusts of the enemy's lies have stolen from me. He daily binds up my wounds and tends to the deepest needs of my soul.

When I realized my need for healing with regard to my sexual identity, I had to ask Him the question, "Why me, Father?" His response. "Why not you?" We were never promised a bed of roses in this life. When we follow Christ, we take up a cross and follow Him. I believe mankind brought sickness into the world when Adam and Eve sinned. Our God is so awesome that He uses sickness to bring about good in our lives and to bring glory—a Light to the world—to Himself. "Why would you allow me to go through Parkinson's, Lord?" Again He answers, "Why not you?"

If the Lord does not heal me in this lifetime, He will heal me in the next. Either way, I win. My daily goal is to use Parkinson's for the kingdom of God, to bring light to the darkness of this world by reminding people that our God wastes nothing we bring to Him. He does not waste our sorrow. He does not waste our pain. He does not even waste our failure. His name is precious to me. His names are life to me. His name is a shelter for my soul. Whether I live or die, nothing changes with Him. We all die. The question becomes, do all really live or do we succumb to the whims of our ailments and maladies? I choose to live and die with my eyes fixed on Jesus while allowing Him to use my sickness for His glory and for the good of others. That truth alone lifts me right out of the middle of nowhere and plants my feet on the Solid Rock of faith in Jesus Christ. Our God.

> And we know that God causes all things to work together for good to those who love God, to those who are called according to His purpose.
>
> — ROMANS 8:28

> The name of the Lord is a strong tower;
> The righteous runs into it and is safe.
>
> — PROVERBS 18:10

20

I HAVE MY SWORD

It is written, "Man shall not live by bread alone, but by every word of God."

— JESUS CHRIST, LUKE 4:4 NKJV

I Have My Sword
Words & Music: Dennis Jernigan
July 1, 2016

When fear surrounds
I will not be afraid
I'll put on the armor
And bear Your name
Once lost, now found
Now free from sin and shame
I bear the cross
With passion's holy flame

I have my Sword!

Your Living Word!
The sound of freedom!
Sweetest ever heard!
By faith I'll stand
And lean into the fight!
And darkness bows
Before the Light
Knowing the blood has satisfied!

Where sin abounds
There is much more grace
Perfect love has conquered
Taken my place
Though battle rages
I'll keep running this race
Until I run
Into my King's embrace

I have my Sword!
Your Living Word!
The sound of freedom!
Sweetest ever heard!
By faith I'll stand
And lean into the fight!
And darkness bows
Before the Light
Knowing the blood has satisfied!

The story behind this song is very simple. I woke up the morning of July 16, 2016, with the awareness that I needed a new song for our free monthly song giveaway. As I began to ponder which new song I needed to release, I felt an urging of the Holy Spirit that He would give me a new song...that very day! I had no idea what the song might entail until a friend asked me to review a movie trailer she had created depicting the need for training in spiritual warfare. Coupled with the fact that in three days we would be celebrating our nation's independence from tyranny, I was overwhelmed with the need for the body of Christ to wake up to the reality of spiritual warfare. In the film trailer, much of the action depicted entailed sword fighting as a visual representation of a spiritual truth. God's Word is my Sword. As I meditated on that truth, this song was born. It is a hymn of declaration and faith.

Spiritual warfare is real. The truth of the Lord God Almighty is opposed by the lies of the enemy, Satan, the liar. The goal of this liar is to cause us to be tempted into living our lives by anything other than the Word of God. A wise believer understands this reality, receives the weapons of that warfare from the Lord…from His Word…and lives an abundant life. In fact, I surmise that the Word of God is THE weapon of weapons in our spiritual arsenal. In God's Word, we have everything we need to vanquish the lies of the enemy. In God's Word, we have been given the keys to the kingdom of God by which we are able to unlock the prisons of the lies we have believed and find freedom for our minds. The reason I say freedom for our minds is because of the simple, fundamental truth of spiritual warfare: The battleground is our mind. The war is won or lost by what we believe about who God is and about who He says we are.

> For the word of God is living and active and sharper than any two-edged sword, and piercing as far as the division of soul and spirit, of both joints and marrow, and able to judge the thoughts and intentions of the heart.
>
> — HEBREWS 4:12

When I am feeling something negative, I immediately trace

that feeling back to the thought that put it in motion. If that thought does not align with the Word of God, I lop it off with the truth of God's Word, replace it with the truth of God's Word, and move on down the road! Let's be honest here. Most of our battles are connected to what we perceive to be our identity. I can either allow the liar and the current humanistic ideology to determine my identity or I can allow the Word of God to determine who I am. As I have said many times in my life, one of my personal rules concerning my thought life is this: Dennis Jernigan does not get to call himself something His Father does not call him.

> Finally, brethren, whatever is true, whatever is honorable, whatever is right, whatever is pure, whatever is lovely, whatever is of good repute, if there is any excellence and if anything worthy of praise, dwell on these things.
>
> — PHILIPPIANS 4:8

In order to renew my mind, which I believe is spiritual warfare birthed in intimacy with Christ, I must recognize the real battleground. As I have already mentioned, the real battleground of every human that has ever existed or ever will exist is the mind. It is imperative that I understand this truth if I am to walk in victory or settle for victimhood. Yes, I battle the physical malady of Parkinson's. My physical body would have me focus all my attention on the physical pain and weakness, but I have come to understand that the real battle is for my thoughts, so I use the Word of God to overcome the suffering of the flesh by filling my head with the truth of God's Word. This does not necessarily ease my physical pain or suffering, but it does give me the vantage point of the big picture. God wastes nothing, and, living or dying, I am with Him! I use the sword of God's Word to take every thought captive because I understand the true essence of where the ward is taking place.

> For though we walk in the flesh, we do not war according to the flesh, for the weapons of our warfare are not of the flesh, but divinely powerful for the destruction of fortresses. We are destroying speculations and every lofty thing raised up against the knowledge of God, and we are taking every thought captive to the obedience of Christ, and we are ready to punish all disobedience, whenever your obedience is complete.
>
> — 2 CORINTHIANS 10:3-6

Yes, I suffer physically due to my sickness, but I am bound and determined to use even the sickness for the kingdom of God. Yes, I am physically weak a great deal of the time, but I boast in my weakness that God might be glorified. My weakness is then replaced by the strength of God. Another great paradox and mystery of knowing God: When I am weak, He is strong.

> Finally, be strong in the Lord and in the strength of His might. Put on the full armor of God, so that you will be able to stand firm against the schemes of the devil. For our struggle is not against flesh and blood, but against the rulers, against the powers, against the world forces of this darkness, against the spiritual forces of wickedness in the heavenly places. Therefore, take up the full armor of God, so that you will be able to resist in the evil day, and having done everything, to stand firm. Stand firm therefore, having girded your loins with truth, and having put on the breastplate of righteousness, and having shod your feet with the preparation of the gospel of peace; in addition to all, taking up the shield of faith with which you will be able to

extinguish all the flaming arrows of the evil one. And take the helmet of, and the sword of the Spirit, which is the word of God.

— EPHESIANS 6:10-17

If I understand that the battle is for my thoughts and is waged in my mind, I must also understand that God has not left me defenseless in this battle. We have been given everything we need to defeat the lies of the enemy. I won't belabor the point. Here is your spiritual armor and arsenal, overcomer:

LOINS GIRDED WITH TRUTH

Why the loins? In a physical sense, this represents the conduit for creating new life. Our God is all about life and wants us to live it abundantly in spite of our circumstances. Let truth guard your spiritual life.

BREASTPLATE OF RIGHTEOUSNESS

This covers our heart. We are to guard our hearts with all diligence. This simply means understanding that we stand unashamed regardless of our past because Jesus became sin on our behalf and made us, as new creations, the righteousness of God! Guard your heart by proclaiming who and Whose you are...often!

SHOD YOUR FEET WITH THE PREPARATION OF THE GOSPEL OF PEACE

Wherever you walk in this life, you are standing on the holy ground of who you are in Christ and have been equipped to tell your story—the Good News/Gospel—of what Christ has done for you.

THE SHIELD OF FAITH

Hebrews 11:1 says, "Now faith is the assurance of things hoped for, the conviction of things not seen." This shield is like a force field around your mind, which is used to dispel the fiery darts (the lies) of the liar! All you need is a mustard seed's worth!

THE SWORD OF THE SPIRIT, WHICH IS THE WORD OF GOD

Jesus used the Word of God to put down the lies and the temptations the liar presented to Him. We have been given the mind of Christ. That means we are equipped to do the same thing!

We really have been given everything we need to overcome the lies of the enemy. And the best news of all? Jesus is our Mighty Warrior who has already sealed and ensured the ultimate victory for us!

> Grace and peace be multiplied to you in the knowledge of God and of Jesus our Lord; seeing that His divine power has granted to us everything pertaining to life and godliness, through the true knowledge of Him who called us by His own glory and excellence.
>
> — 2 PETER 1:2-3

Looking back on my life to this point gives me a better perspective on what I am facing now. Throughout my past, when I faced middle-of-nowhere moments, I was rescued and found solid ground for my thoughts by putting off the lies of the enemy and by wielding the sword of God's Word. He is faithful and true to His Word, and he keeps His promises. He did not promise me an easy journey, but He did promise me He would never leave me or forsake me.

> For by these He has granted to us His precious and magnificent promises, so that by them you may become partakers of the divine nature, having escaped the corruption that is in the world by lust. Now for this very reason also, applying all diligence, in your faith supply moral excellence, and in your moral excellence, knowledge, and in your knowledge, self-control, and in your self-control, perseverance, and in your perseverance, godliness, and in your godliness, brotherly kindness, and in your brotherly kindness, love. For if these qualities are yours and are increasing, they render you neither useless nor unfruitful in the true knowledge of our Lord Jesus Christ.
>
> — 2 PETER 1:4-8

Reality is that I still experience persecution, the pain of a mortal body, and fear. Reality is that I sometimes feel like giving up. Reality is as long as I live in this human body, I will face storms and middle-of-nowhere moments. But the greater reality is this: I win. I am more than a conqueror. I am soaked in and surrounded by the love and presence of God. And I have my sword…

21

I REBUKE THE DARKNESS

"People are like stained - glass windows. They sparkle and shine when the sun is out, but when the darkness sets in, their true beauty is revealed only if there is a light from within."

— ELISABETH KUBLER-ROSS

For our struggle is not against flesh and blood, but against the rulers, against the powers, against the world forces of this darkness, against the spiritual forces of wickedness in the heavenly places.

— EPHESIANS 6:12

I Rebuke the Darkness
Words & Music: Dennis Jernigan
August 3, 2013

We are at war!
We are in conflict

With the darkness and its principalities!
We are at war!
In constant conflict
In a world that, day by day, grows more deceived!

So get your heart prepared to fight!
No matter what, follow the Light!
So let us boldly face the night
And keep our eyes fixed on the Light!

I rebuke the darkness in the name of Jesus!
I rebuke the Liar! I rebuke the lies!
I rebuke the darkness by the blood of Jesus!
Call down holy fire! Open blinded eyes!

Remember to put on the armor!
Let the helmet of salvation guard your mind!
Take up the sword of the Spirit!
You are the righteousness of God through Jesus Christ!
Do not lose heart! Just stand and fight!
You're not alone! Look to the Light!

When you're knocked down, stand up again!
Though live or die, we will still win!

I rebuke the darkness in the name of Jesus!
I rebuke the Liar! I rebuke the lies!
I rebuke the darkness by the blood of Jesus!
Call down holy fire! Open blinded eyes!

Jesus! Jesus! The mighty name of Jesus!
Jesus! Jesus! The Way! The Truth! The Life!
Jesus! Jesus! The mighty name of Jesus!

Jesus! Jesus! The Way! The Truth! The Life!

I rebuke the darkness in the name of Jesus!
I rebuke the Liar! I rebuke the lies!
I rebuke the darkness by the blood of Jesus!
Call down holy fire! Open blinded eyes!

This song was born after a long period of intense attacks by the enemy in 2013. Everything that could go wrong did go wrong! Multiple cars broke down. House repairs were needed. My wife broke her leg and required a hospital stay of five days and a recovery time of more than eight weeks. On top of these things, add the constant barrage of the enemy from the world that says I am wrong for proclaiming freedom from homosexuality (just read some of the comments left on my YouTube testimony site). In addition, a film was being produced about my life, along with a recording of my songs by young Christian artists, and the artists willing to be associated with the documentary were few and far between.

What sent me over the edge to receive this song? Driving my daughter home from a ministry she had taken part in over that summer in Ft. Lauderdale, Florida, back to Oklahoma, the car died 125 miles from home on a very busy I-40! We had to be towed home, and I walked in the house to discover the downstairs bathroom had flooded from a leak from somewhere Upstairs! A definite middle-of-nowhere moment for me and my family! A sobering time of darkness, for sure.

Two other factors, not of the dire nature, also helped lead to the writing of this song. On the Florida trip, I had decided to finally read *Waking the Dead* by John Eldredge. It's all about how the enemy is the enemy and he desires to get us to lose heart! That was me! I was quickly losing heart! And then while on the trip, my daughter asked to go see *Man of Steel,* and God spoke to me through that film! I came away blessed by the Lord deep in my heart. It actually left me feeling reborn in a way. Following are some of the quotes I gleaned from the film that God used to help me rebuke the darkness in my life!

Concerning my destiny: Jonathan Kent (Clark's adoptive father) says to Clark, "You are my son, but somewhere out there you have another father, and he sent you here for a reason. And even if it takes you the rest of your life, you owe it to yourself to find out what that reason is."

Darkness is dispelled by the Light of Truth. Even when darkness surrounds us, we are still people of purpose and destiny. Just as with Clark's father, our Father says so! Darkness is dispelled by the Light of God's Word.

Clark says to Lois, "My father believed that if the world found out who I really was, they'd reject me, out of fear. He was convinced that the world wasn't ready. What do you think?"

Reality is that this world and the Liar do reject me and try to persuade me to lose heart and give up. Bad things do happen. The crucifixion of Christ happened. I have been crucified with Christ. He rose. I will rise. Darkness rebuked.

Concerning the call upon my life to declare my redemption through Jesus: Jor-El (Clark's birth father) says to Kal-el (Superman), "You will give the people an ideal to strive towards. They will race behind you, they will stumble, they will fall. But in time, they will join you in the sun. In time, you will help them accomplish wonders."

I have been called to be an ambassador for Christ. Period. Regardless of persecution. Regardless of Parkinson's. Regardless of whatever, I am redeemed and I am called and compelled to do so. Darkness vanquished!

Concerning how alone I feel at times: Pre-teen Clark Kent says to his mother, Martha, "The world's too big, Mom." Martha

Kent replies, "Then make it small. Focus on my voice. Pretend it's an island out in the ocean. Can you see it?"

Vanquishing the darkness of the lies of the enemy requires a different point of view. A kingdom point of view. A Jesus point of view. I can either focus on the insurmountable mountain of darkness I see before me, or I can focus on the molehill that darkness is when compared to the mountain of God's light!

What I gleaned from that film was unexpected. God speaks in any way God chooses, and for some reason, He chose to use that film to break through the darkness of my life in that moment. I know I am not Superman. But being raised on a farm, I know what one seed that falls to the earth can accomplish. Bottom line? I must remember that the enemy is at work against me...but the Lord is for me.

I must remember that God has called me and that, according to Romans 11:29, "...the gifts and the calling of God are irrevocable." I will fight because I am a warrior of the Kingdom fighting for the King. Because of my authority in Christ to do so, I rebuke the darkness of humanistic thinking. I rebuke the darkness of Parkinson's. I rebuke the darkness of self-pity. I rebuke the darkness of being defined by my feelings. I rebuke the darkness of the lies of the enemy. I rebuke the darkness and put it in its place. Out of my mind and under my feet. I rebuked the darkness...and this song was born.

22

UNSHAKABLE

"There is nothing we could do of greater importance than to have fortified in our individual lives an unshakable conviction that Jesus is the Christ, the living Son of the living God."

— GORDON B. HINCKLEY

"Endurance is not just the ability to bear a hard thing, but to turn it into glory."

— WILLIAM BARCLAY

Unshakable
Words & Music: Dennis Jernigan
February 12, 2016

Once more the time has come
For lies to be undone
Real hope stands on Solid Ground

All other hopes come crashing down!
Kingdoms built on strength of man
Such kingdoms cannot stand
Built on sand not Solid Ground
Such kingdoms all come crashing down!

Everything that can be will be shaken!
Everything that can be is coming down!
Everything that can be will be shaken!
Except the Kingdom built on Solid Ground!

Unshakable! This Kingdom!
Unshakable! This King!
Unshakable! This Kingdom!
Unshakable! The redeemed!
Unshakable! Kingdom come!
Unshakable! Will be done!
Unshakable! Kingdom come in me!

This present darkness may
Bring fear to cloud the way
Calling evil what is good
Making idols where a cross once stood!
Hearts of stone that will not turn
Melt away like grass when burned
Make sure of your heart's desire!
Our God is the All-Consuming Fire!

Everything that can be will be shaken!
Everything that can be is coming down!
Everything that can be will be shaken!
Except the Kingdom built on Solid Ground!

Unshakable! This Kingdom!
Unshakable! This King!
Unshakable! This Kingdom!
Unshakable! The redeemed!
Unshakable! Kingdom come!
Unshakable! Will be done!
Unshakable! Kingdom come in me!

One day every knee will bow!
One day every tongue will shout!
Jesus Christ! Jesus Christ is King!
This very day my knee I bow!
This very day my tongue will shout!
Kingdom come! Kingdom come in me!
Come in me!

Unshakable! This Kingdom!
Unshakable! This King!
Unshakable! This Kingdom!
Unshakable! The redeemed!
Unshakable! Kingdom come!
Unshakable! Will be done!
Unshakable! Kingdom come in me!

This song had been brewing in my heart since hearing my spiritual mentor, Jack Taylor, speak on the kingdom of God, specifically from Hebrews 12. God truly is in control regardless of the cultural state of our world, regardless of who is the leader of the political world, regardless of any circumstance I may encounter. What helped bring the song to fruition was coupling what Jack's words had stirred in my heart with a very real circumstance facing one of my sons.

That very week, he found out his company was downsizing drastically and his position was being cut. He was shaken. This song came out with several components. Boasting in God. Warning the church to be ready for the shaking that is certainly coming. Proclaiming Jesus Christ as King over all. Encouragement to the body that our King and His kingdom cannot be shaken. That is wonderful news!

> See to it that you do not refuse Him who is speaking. For if those did not escape when they refused him who warned them on earth, much less will we escape who turn away from Him who warns from heaven. And His voice shook the earth then, but now He has promised, saying, "Yet once more I will shake not only the earth, but also the heaven." This expression, "Yet once more," denotes the removing of those things which can be shaken, as of created things, so that those things which cannot be shaken may remain. Therefore, since we receive a kingdom which cannot be shaken, let us show gratitude, by which we may offer to God an acceptable service with reverence and awe; for our God is a consuming fire.
>
> — HEBREWS 12:25-29

Life is a marathon and marathons require endurance. Reality is that life is full of moments of great shaking...tremors of pain and suffering and lack and betrayals and temptations and all manner of things the enemy will try to use to cause us to lose heart and give up the running of the race. But we have been given grace to run the entire race and finish well with joy in our hearts.

One night several years ago, Melinda and I were sitting in our chairs (yes, we have grandpa and grandma chairs), watching a favorite TV show when the entire atmosphere began to vibrate without warning. My first thought was that a military helicopter was hovering much too close to our rooftop. We expected the aircraft to move on, but it felt like it was getting closer and closer. Soon, the entire room began to vibrate. The entire house began to shudder violently. Walls and floors began to creak and moan. Melinda and I were looking at one another, frozen in fear as we shook in our chairs. It felt as if the house was swaying slightly back and forth; waves of power were surging through both house and the air we were gasping for.

After about 40 seconds, the shaking, trembling, shuddering, thunderous-sounding "whatever the heck that was" stopped as suddenly as it had begun. Melinda and I sat there looking at one another in bewilderment. We were in shock. As we gripped the arms of our chairs, we spoke in unison, "Earthquake!" The local news noted the quake had registered 4.8 on the Richter scale! As soon as we felt safe to do so, we went around the house looking for signs of damage.

Pictures were crooked. Some had fallen from the walls. A crack developed in the ceiling of our bedroom along the wall where the wall and ceiling met. The floor tiles in our bedroom cracked and some had even warped upward, looking like cracks of ice forced upward from an ice floe in an ice-packed river. As we ventured outside to survey the damage to our home, we noticed that the faces of many of the bricks on the two brick chimneys had shattered and fallen like some weird snow all over the back deck and yard. For 40 seconds, we experienced a physical picture of what a spiritual earthquake looks like!

The shaking trials of my life may be different than yours, but we all must go through them. Even our earthly house received minor damage, it held firm because its foundation was on solid ground. Whatever could be shaken had been shaken, but what could not be shaken was left standing.

God allows and sometimes causes the shaking times in our

lives in order to help us see our need for placing our faith and building our spiritual house on the Solid Rock of Jesus Christ. This is why a kingdom point of view is vital to living an abundant life even while enduring the violent upheaval life brings our way. The kingdom of God is unshakable, and we are to seek that kingdom first and foremost if we are to walk in our true identities in Christ. And just how do we seek first the kingdom of God? We seek first the King!

My life was shaken by the temptation of same-sex attraction. On November 7, 1981, Jesus stopped that shaking when He rescued me from the lies concerning my identity while simultaneously planting my feet on Solid Ground

My life was shaken by persecution and times when people tried to silence me. My life has been shaken by vile insults and offensive threats. What was left after these times of shaking? The ability to identify more with Christ, the ability to bless those who curse me, the grace to forgive those who would do me harm, the ability to love those who hate me. The kingdom point of view, in a sense, is that I am commanded to love even if I don't agree with those who would silence me.

My life was shaken by grief and loss, but what was left after the loss of my grandmother and the loss of my dad was the eternal truth that I will see them again someday soon.

My life has been shaken by the ravages of Parkinson's: The loss of a major portion of my ability to sing, the loss of physical strength in my right hand to the point my three right-most fingers seldom work anymore (you should see the remaining thumb and forefinger of my right hand as they try to compensate for the loss of their companions when I am playing the piano, LOL!), by the constant what-ifs having such an illness brings to one's mind.

What cannot be shaken is the fact that I can still worship God with my voice. It may be a whisper of its former self, but it is even more passionate and precious than before.

What cannot be shaken is the fact that I still have the use of two fingers on my right hand and the reality that, should I lose all physical ability someday, I will still be able to praise God with my entire being.

What cannot be shaken when fear rises is the fact that God is my constant Companion and that He loves me with all He is.

Let's review the last portion of that passage from Hebrews I quoted earlier. Hebrews 12:28 says, "Therefore, since we receive a kingdom which cannot be shaken, let us show gratitude, by which we may offer to God an acceptable service with reverence and awe..." May I suggest that we walk in gratitude for what we DO have and not focus on what we don't have? The latter always leads to despair and constant sorrow.

Hebrews 12:29 gives us all we need to know about how to deal with the shaking times of life. It reads, "...for our God is a consuming fire." I believe that fire is the power of His love to burn through the things of this earth in whatever way He chooses. He is God and He can do and use whatever He likes to get our attention. The jealousy He has for us, to know us intimately, burns with the fire of passion He has for each of us.

His love, like a fire, burned away the shackles of my sin. His love, like a fire, burned through the times or persecution, betrayal, and wounding, leaving me wonderfully able to forgive and bless even those who hate me, leaving my conscience clear and my mind willfully dependent upon Him and His love. His love, like a fire, burned away my grief over the diagnosis of Parkinson's and the subsequent loss of my voice and three fingers, and left me recognizing my need to rest from my labors and to cherish the things most dear to me and my life: My wife, my children, my grandchildren, my family, and my friends.

I am an unshakable child of Almighty God whose only goal in life, at this point, is to leave as large a legacy—a roadmap—of how to live an abundant life as possible for generations to come. I am more determined than ever to use whatever comes into my life for the King and for the Kingdom of God. Let the physical pain come. Let the loss of memory come. Let the loss of stamina come. I will use them all for the King and kingdom because I am unshakable.

REFERENCES

Scripture references are from the New American Standard Bible unless otherwise noted.

The quotations at the beginning of each chapter are found on various websites including azquotes.com, brainyquote.com, goodreads.com, loveathomecares.com, and quotes.net.

Quotes from *Man of Steel*
    This film is based on the DC Comics character Superman.
    Produced by DC Entertainment, Legendary Pictures, Syncopy and Cruel and Unusual Films, and distributed by Warner Bros. Pictures

Jernigan quote in Jamaica Observer:
    jamaicaobserver.com/news/VIDEO--Obama-deceived-on-same-sex-marriage_11518025

Jernigan Exodus International resignation announcement: boxturtlebulletin.com/2012/06/15/45818

For insight into Dennis Jernigan's beliefs about gender identity issues, he suggests you read the following blog by James Emery White: churchandculture.org/blog/2020/2/20/sex-matters

Original Dennis Jernigan songs © Shepherd's Heart Music, Inc./Dennis Jernigan; 7804 W. Fern Mountain Rd., Muskogee, OK 74401; 1-800-877-0406; dennisjernigan.com; Administered by PraiseCharts.com

BECOME A DJ INSIDER

Would you like to receive daily devotions, music, new releases, and exclusive updates from me? Join me on Patreon to become a DJ Insider. Learn more at www.patreon.com/dennisjernigan.

ALSO BY DENNIS JERNIGAN

Non-fiction
Sing Over Me: An Autobiography

Renewing Your Mind: Identity and the Matter of Choice

Daily Devotions for Kingdom Seekers Series

Fiction for Adults
A Thread of Hope

The Short Life

Fantasy for Young Readers
Captured

Sacrifice

Generations

Hide and Seek

The Light Eater

Picture Books
The Incredible Growing Basketball Goal

Daddy's Song

The Christmas Dream

DVD
Sing Over Me: The Dennis Jernigan Documentary

Many other recordings, books, and resources are available at www.dennisjernigan.com.

WHO IS DENNIS JERNIGAN?

Dennis Jernigan is a Kingdom Seeker. On November 7, 1981 he walked out of his old identity and into the Kingdom of God. He began to seek Jesus—the King—and not a ministry, yet ministry has flowed out of his life in world-reaching ways. His songs are sung in tens of thousands of churches around the world each and every week. His story is read and heard and recounted to thousands each month via YouTube, Facebook, dennisjernigan.com, and his many speaking and concert engagements.

Through the years, Dennis has been privileged to work with the likes of Dr. James Dobson, Steve Farrar, Anne Graham Lotz, James Robison, Beth Moore, Max Lucado, and Andy Comiskey and has recorded with Annie Herring, Matthew Ward, Alvin Slaughter, Rebecca St. James, Travis Cottrell, Charlie Hall,

Natalie Grant, Ron Kenoly, Christie Nockels, First Call, and Twila Paris.

Dennis Jernigan's mission statement can be boiled down to this:

> The Spirit of the Lord is upon me, because he anointed me to preach the gospel to the poor. He has sent me to proclaim release to the captives, and recovery of sight to the blind, to set free those who are oppressed, to proclaim the favorable year of the Lord.
>
> — LUKE 4:18-19

Dennis lives with his wife, Melinda, in Muskogee, OK, where they raised their nine children. They are now welcoming many grandchildren.

To book Dennis Jernigan for ministry, call 918-781-1200 or simply email us at mail@dennisjernigan.com.

For more information:
www.dennisjernigan.com
mail@dennisjernigan.com
patreon.com/dennisjernigan

facebook.com/official.dennisjernigan
youtube.com/dennisjernigan
instagram.com/dennisjernigan
twitter.com/dennisjernigan
amazon.com/author/dennisjernigan

www.ingramcontent.com/pod-product-compliance
Lightning Source LLC
Chambersburg PA
CBHW050319120526
44592CB00014B/1976